KIERKEGAARD

FOR BEGINNERS ™

WRITERS AND READERS PUBLISHING, INC.
P.O. Box 461, Village Station
New York, NY 10014

Writers and Readers Limited
9 Cynthia Street
London N1 9JF
England

•

A Writers and Readers Documentary Comic Book
Copyright © 1996
ISBN # 0-86316-192-8 Trade
   3 4 5 6 7 8 9 0

Manufactured in the United States of America

Beginners Documentary Comic Books are published by Writers and Readers Publishing, Inc. Its trademark, consisting of the words "For Beginners, Writers and Readers Documentary Comic Books" and the Writers and Readers logo, is registered in the U. S. Patent and Trademark Office and in other countries.

Writers and Readers—
publishing FOR BEGINNERS™ books
continuously since 1975:

1975: Cuba • 1976: Marx • 1977: Lenin • 1978: Nuclear Power • 1979: Einstein • Freud • 1980: Mao • Trotsky • 1981: Capitalism • 1982: Darwin • Economists • French Revolution • Marx's Kapital • French Revolution • Food • Ecology • 1983: DNA • Ireland • 1984: London • Peace • Medicine • Orwell • Reagan • Nicaragua • Black History • 1985: Marx Diary • 1986: Zen • Psychiatry • Reich • Socialism • Computers • Brecht • Elvis • 1988: Architecture • Sex • JFK • Virginia Woolf • 1990: Nietzsche • Plato • Malcolm X • Judaism • 1991: WW II • Erotica • African History • 1992: Philosophy • Rainforests • Malcolm X • Miles Davis • Islam • Pan Africanism • 1993: Psychiatry • Black Women • Arabs & Israel • Freud • 1994: Babies • Foucault • Heidegger • Hemingway • Classical Music • 1995: Jazz • Jewish Holocaust • Health Care • Domestic Violence • Sartre • United Nations • Black Holocaust • Black Panthers • Martial Arts • History of Clowns • 1996: Opera • Biology • Saussure • UNICEF • Kierkegaard • Addiction & Recovery • I Ching • Buddha • Derrida • Chomsky • McLuhan • Jung • 1997: Lacan • Shakespeare • Structuralism

---

Dedication

TO Josiah "Tink" Thompson
Proto-Kierkegaardian
turned
Crypto-Kierkegaardian

Table of Contents

KIERKEGAARD

FOR BEGINNERS™

WRITTEN AND ILLUSTRATED BY DONALD D. PALMER

Writers and Readers

SØREN KIERKEGAARD (1813-1855)

lived only forty-two years. Yet in his short life, he wrote more than twenty-five books. After his death, his works slipped into obscurity.

I STARTED EARLY!

When they were rediscovered in the twentieth century they revolutionized European thinking and produced the philosophy that came to be known as

EXISTENTIALISM.

Who was this man, and what did he have to say?

THIS IS ABOUT US

In one way, it's surprising anybody reads him, because all his writings are about himself, his father, and his girlfriend.

...BUT THEY TURN OUT TO BE ABOUT YOU AND ME TOO.

*L*et's start our story by talking about Søren's father, Michael.

MICHAEL PEDERSEN KIERKEGAARD (1756-1838) had spent his youth in dire poverty in Denmark's windswept sand dune country of Northern Jutland, where at one moment in his childish despair while tending sheep out on the barren heathland he had raised his little fist to heaven and had cursed God, a major sin in the Lutheran Pietism in which he had been raised.

GUD J HIMMEL ⊙ ⚡💧!!!

As a young man he had come to Copenhagen and parlayed a small saving into a sizeable wealth, steeping himself in books and making smart social connections.

THE KING OF DENMARK WOULD SOMETIMES BE AT THE TABLE WHEN SØREN WAS A SMALL BOY.

Søren Kierkegaard was born in Copenhagen on May 5, 1813, the last of seven children. His mother, Anne Lund Kierkegaard, was his old father's second wife and had been the maid of the first Mrs. Kierkegaard during the period of her final illness.

WAHHH! I'M GOING TO MAKE A BIG FUSS!

There remains the hint of a sexual impropriety between Michael and the maid during the last months of the life of the terminally ill Mrs. Kierkegaard. This sin or some other (perhaps the one from Michael's childhood) had made the old man an overbearing religious penitent who was morbidly fanatical in his belief that he had offended God.

I AM GUILTY!

*I*n a certain sense, young Søren was sacrificed on the altar of his father's religiosity, or he <u>almost</u> was, just as young Isaac of the Biblical story was almost sacrificed on his father's altar.

It is no mere coincidence that Kierkegaard was fascinated by the story of Abraham and Isaac all his life. This story, taken as a metaphor, illuminates much of Kierkegaard's adult behavior.

FOR EXAMPLE, HE BELIEVED THAT HIS "NORMALITY" HAD BEEN SACRIFICED ON A RELIGIOUS ALTAR. HIS SPECIFIC MISSION—BASICALLY A RELIGIOUS ONE—PREVENTED HIM FROM BEING LIKE OTHER PEOPLE. IT PRECLUDED MARRIAGE, PARENTHOOD, FAMILY LIFE, AND A CAREER.

Despite his morbid obsession, Michael recognized his son's genius and tried to nurture it. Even though Michael was self-educated, he was very knowledgeable, and he took much of young Søren's instruction into his own hands.

> ... AND THEN THE BISHOP SAID....

He would have the boy eavesdrop on his dinner parties with the elite of Copenhagen, and afterward he would make Søren sit in the empty chair of each guest and set forth the argument which that person had espoused during the dinner.

> AND WHAT'S THAT?
> UUHH, THE EIFFEL TOWER
> IMPOSSIBLE. IT HASN'T BEEN BUILT YET.

He would teach Søren geography by taking his hand and strolling through the living room with him pretending it was a foreign country and making him name famous sights that they would "see" in that country. Søren was sent to Latin School with instructions from his father to bring home the <u>third</u> best grade.

It's easy for a genius to earn the <u>best</u> grade, but to get the third best, he must learn psychology. He must figure out who the second and fourth smartest boys are and place his own work between theirs.

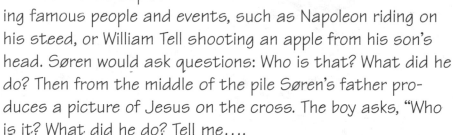

*H*is father would show the little boy colored illustrations from a stack of cards depicting famous people and events, such as Napoleon riding on his steed, or William Tell shooting an apple from his son's head. Søren would ask questions: Who is that? What did he do? Then from the middle of the pile Søren's father produces a picture of Jesus on the cross. The boy asks, "Who is it? What did he do? Tell me....

Why were people so bad to him?" The father tells his son, "This is the Saviour of the world. He was killed by those whom he would save." Years later Kierkegaard wrote, "As a child I was sternly and seriously brought up in Christianity. Humanly speaking, it was a crazy upbringing."

AS A CHILD I HAD ALREADY BEEN MADE INTO AN OLD MAN.

There is a passage in the Bible according to which

"the sins of the father will be visited upon the sons."

The Kierkegaard family mythology interpreted this as morbidly as possible to mean that as payment for his sins, old Michael would have to bury all seven of his children before his own death. (The number seven has always had a mystical significance in the Bible.) And sure enough, one by one, the children died off, leaving only Søren and his brother, Peter. Therefore Søren was totally amazed when at two A.M. on August 9, 1838, his father died at eighty-two years of age. Søren had simply assumed that he would die young and had made no plans for his life. His first published work was called,

"Papers from One Surviving."

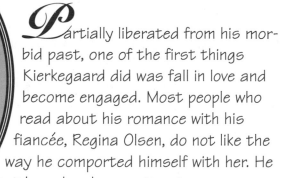

artially liberated from his morbid past, one of the first things Kierkegaard did was fall in love and become engaged. Most people who read about his romance with his fiancée, Regina Olsen, do not like the way he comported himself with her. He met her when he was twenty-one and she was fourteen, that is to say, three years before he could properly court her. He spent those three years well, ingratiating himself with her family, finding out everything about her he could, placing himself in a position to influence her aesthetic taste, and even befriending her boyfriend, Fritz Schlegel, using his position of confidence to undermine poor Fritz.

In his pseudonymous fictional story, "Diary of a Seducer," Kierkegaard tells of the seduction of a young woman by a man who studies her every gesture. The reader of the story realizes that the woman is doomed because of the totality of the seducer's plan. Similarly, those who know the thoroughness of Kierkegaard's plotting to win Regina feel that she, too, was snared before she had a chance to react. Sure enough, when Regina turned seventeen, Søren wooed her and won her. The engagement party took place, and the announcement was published.

𝒦ierkegaard seemed happy with his victory and was well on his way to becoming a solidly entrenched member of the bourgeois establishment, when suddenly for no reason he shared with anyone else, he broke the engagement. In his diary he wrote that he had done so because "God had vetoed the marriage." Regina was heartbroken and begged him to return to her. Her father humiliated himself pleading Regina's case. Kierkegaard was intractable and cold. He allowed himself to be seen frolicking in questionable neighborhoods of Copenhagen.

Then he disappeared from Denmark and sneaked off to Berlin, where he enrolled at the University in a course on Hegelian philosophy under the prominent Professor Schelling, and where his classmates included none other than Friedrich Engels, Ludwig Feuerbach and Michael Bukunin—each of whom would later exert a powerful influence on European thought.

After the termination of the academic quarter, he returned to Copenhagen, but when he thought he saw Regina nod at him in church, he fled to Berlin again. While in Berlin this second time he wrote one of his greatest books, Fear and Trembling, his book about Abraham and Isaac, and it contained a secret message for Regina.

In one of the book's many interpretations of Abraham's story, Kierkegaard imagines Abraham as pretending before Isaac that it was not God who had demanded Isaac's death, but that Abraham himself desired it because he was an idolater and a murderer. Abraham feigns being a criminal so that Isaac, with his dying breath, would curse Abraham and not God. So, Kierkegaard had acted like a cad in order that Regina would not blame God for the sacrifice of the love between her and Søren!

Moreover, Kierkegaard wrote in his diary that by assuming responsibility for the break, he would free Regina to love again. Yet, when he returned from Berlin and discovered that she was engaged to Fritz Schlegel, Kierkegaard was beside himself with jealousy and a sense of loss. Some time later he wrote in his journal,

(Regina married Schlegel, who was made governor of the Danish Virgin Islands. He and Regina had a good life there. But after Schlegel's death, Regina made it clear that she still loved the now long-dead Kierkegaard.)

"IF I HAD FAITH, I WOULD HAVE REMAINED WITH REGINA."

He went to his grave still love-sick.

It seems that Kierkegaard had only three significant human relationships that had a major impact on his life:

one with his father,   one with Regina Olsen,

and one with the editor of the popular comical newspaper, <u>The Corsair</u>.

This was a vulgar satirical journal that purported to serve liberal political causes by mocking the haute-bourgeoisie of Copenhagen. In fact, it was at least as much of a titillating peep-show for the gossip-mongering voyeurs and would-be imitators of the upper-middle class that the newspaper parodied. Its editor, Meïr Goldschmidt, spared no one his barbs, <u>except</u> Søren Kierkegaard, whom he greatly admired.

*W*hen one of Kierkegaard's books was reviewed favorably in <u>The Corsair</u>, Kierkegaard wrote a sarcastic letter to the editor, saying that being praised in <u>The Corsair</u> was a major insult, and that he would much more prefer to have his book attacked, which would be tantamount to a compliment. The humiliated Goldschmidt began a daily attack on poor Kierkegaard, which was relentless and devastating.

A COMPLIMENT FROM *YOU*, MY DEAR SIR, IS AN INSULT

TOUCHÉ

I'LL GET YOU FOR THIS

By then Kierkegaard's weak spine had given him stooped posture and his skinny legs with cuffs that were too high to be stylish made him an easy target for the caricaturist's pen.

He became a laugh-
ing stock through-
out Denmark and
was sneered at by
the genteel folk and
insulted by street
urchins and louts
wherever he went.
Goldschmidt
became ashamed of
himself, but the
mockery he began
lasted long after
The Corsair folded.
Kierkegaard tried to
put a brave face on
it, but the "Corsair
affair" was surely
the second-most
painful event in his
life.

In his last years, Kierkegaard abandoned his "indirect communication" and attacked the official Danish Lutheran Church in a most direct manner, further alienating what few friends and supporters he had.

LEMONADE (FORMERLY WHISKY)

According to Kierkegaard, primitive Christianity had been a spiritual revolution that had challenged the status quo and had therefore been an <u>offense</u> to all complacency. But the contemporary Church was the very symbol of self-satisfied bourgeois smugness, so he criticized it relentlessly at every occasion.

He called what the Church was preaching "lemonade twaddle." He eventually printed pamphlets at his own expense and passed them out the way religious zealots often do in the streets of our own cities. (The pamphlets, however, were much more articulate than those of today's typical religious pamphleteer, and all the words were spelled correctly!)

THE WHIRLED IS CUMIN TO AND EN

JESUS

Here are some short examples:

ABRACADABRA! AMEN, AMEN, WORLD WITHOUT END, AMEN! ALL HONOR TO THE PRIESTS!.... THIS IS THE SECRET OF "CHRISTENDOM."

ONE CANNOT LIVE OFF OF NOTHING. THIS ONE HEARS SO OFTEN, ESPECIALLY FROM PRIESTS.... AND PRECISELY THE PRIESTS PERFORM THIS TRICK: CHRISTIANITY ACTUALLY DOES NOT EXIST—YET THEY LIVE OFF OF IT.

THIS HAS TO BE SAID; SO BE IT NOW SAID. WHOEVER THOU ART, WHATEVER IN OTHER RESPECTS THY LIFE MAY BE MY FRIEND, BY CEASING TO TAKE PART IN THE PUBLIC WORSHIP OF GOD, AS IT NOW IS (WITH THE CLAIM THAT IT IS THE CHRISTIANITY OF THE NEW TESTAMENT), THOU HAST CONSTANTLY ONE GUILT THE LESS, AND THAT A GREAT ONE: THOU DOST NOT TAKE PART IN TREATING GOD AS A FOOL.

Kierkegaard was passionately involved in this polemic when, on October 2, 1855, he fell to the street paralyzed. A month and a half later he was dead. There was a near riot at his funeral, as a number of angry theology students at the university were outraged at the way the Church tried to take over in death the man who had opposed it so bitterly with his last breath.

He had wanted to have written on his tombstone simply,

"**The Individual**,"

but instead his stone reads,

"**Søren Aabye Kierkegaard
Born the 5th of May, 1813
Died the 11th of November 1855**."

At least the last name is appropriate. In Danish it means "graveyard."

INDIRECT COMMUNICATION

Kierkegaard's final illness coincided with the moment that he had exhausted the last of his dead father's money. Kierkegaard never really held down a job in his life, but perhaps we can call him a professional writer. He seems to have spent the greatest part of his waking life at his writing desk, and he certainly produced a large number of books in the few years that he lived. (However, it's lucky his father left him a large sum to live off of, because his books were not exactly best sellers.)

What did Kierkegaard write about? About a certain kind of **TRUTH** that he called "subjective truth" or "existential truth." This truth is, according too him, the most important kind of truth, but unfortunately it cannot be communicated directly. It is composed of deep insights or revelations or choices about an individual's life, and they are different in the case of each individual. Kierkegaard finds himself in the paradoxical position of wanting to <u>write books</u> about these truths—that is, of wanting to communicate that which cannot be communicated. Therefore, he develops and employs a <u>theory</u> of <u>indirect communication</u>.

*K*ierkegaard derives much of his inspiration for this theory from his favorite philosopher, old Socrates of Athens (469-399 B.C.) In his discussions, ostensibly recorded by his disciple Plato, Socrates' form of communication is seen to be one of **IRONY**.

HE RARELY SAYS EXACTLY WHAT HE MEANS.

He overstates, understates, misstates, poeticizes, and mythologizes. The classical example of Socrates' irony was his assertion of his own ignorance.

When informed that the oracle at Delphi (spokesperson for the gods) had called Socrates the wisest man in Athens, Socrates claimed to be stunned. How could he be the wisest man in Athens if he knew nothing? However, upon consideration, Socrates concluded that he was indeed wiser than other people because, though he knew nothing, he <u>knew</u> that he knew nothing.

I KNOW NOTHING!

WHICH IS A HELLAVA LOT MORE THAN YOU KNOW

*O*ther people also knew nothing, but thought they knew something. Socrates' ironic claim of ignorance was used, of course, to undermine the arrogant pretense to knowledge by his opponents. We know how devastating his irony could be. By the middle of one of the Platonic dialogues, <u>Alcibiades,</u> Socrates has reduced one of his adversaries to tears. Alcibiades asks,

"SOCRATES, WHAT HAVE YOU DONE TO ME? I NO LONGER KNOW WHO I AM."

According to Kierkegaard, Socrates "approached each man individually, deprived him of everything, and sent him away empty handed." What Socrates taught had no objective content, rather, Socrates became the negative condition whereby learners learned something about themselves. Kierkegaard wrote his Master's thesis (really equivalent to our Doctoral dissertation) on Socrates, and he called it <u>The Concept of Irony</u>.

Once he had received the Master's degree, he liked to think of himself as

"the Master of Irony."

Kierkegaard and Socrates were not the only ones who had "mastered irony." So had the Jesus of the Synoptic Gospels (Matthew, Mark and Luke). It is noteworthy that in the first three Gospels Jesus rarely ever "tells it like it is," rather he preaches using an indirect form of communication that Kierkegaard takes to be essential and not just incidental to his teaching. For example, whenever Jesus is asked about the kingdom of God, he speaks in parables. In Matthew 13 alone, there are six such parables.

(Heaven is like a farmer planting crops, it is like yeast in bread, it is like a treasure hidden in a field, it is like a buyer of pearls, it is like a fisherman's net.)

Jesus uses indirect communication in a marvelous variety of ways. Not only do we see it in the parables

"The kingdom of heaven is like a mustard seed."

but in the harsh sayings

"Let the dead bury their dead",

the sarcasm

"It is as possible for a rich man to enter paradise as it is for a camel to pass through the eye of a needle",

in the bizarre actions

the condemnation of the fig tree: "Let no man eat fruit of thee forever more",

and in the poetry

"The kingdom of God is within you".

According to Kierkegaard, Jesus's method of communicating is unbalancing. It destabilizes the smug complacency that stands between the individual and the truth. Jesus's method is essential to his goal. What Jesus "teaches" cannot be taught in some other more objective manner. The listener is forced to confront the full paradoxical power of "the lesson" and, in doing so, is forced to confront himself or herself. So it was with old Socrates too.

Kierkegaard imitates the methods of Socrates and Jesus in choosing to communicate indirectly and ironically.

I'M CONFUSED...

He does so by writing all of his philosophical works secretly, publishing them under pseudonyms and then disclaiming all responsibility for their content. Kierkegaard employs fourteen different pseudonyms in his work, including names like "Victor Eremita" (Victor the Hermit), "Johannes de silentio" (John the Silent), "Constantin Constantius" (Constantin the Constant), "Johannes Climacus" (John Climax or John the Ladder), "Anti-Climacus" (Anticlimax), "Nicolaus Notabene" (Nicolaus Note-well), and "Hilarius Bookbinder." Each of these authors has his own personality, style, and outlook on life. When Kierkegaard finally admitted (what everyone knew by then) that he was the author of the pseudonymous works, he claimed:

IN THE PSEUDONYMOUS WORKS THERE IS NOT A SINGLE WORD WHICH IS MINE. I HAVE NO OPINION ABOUT THESE WORKS EXCEPT AS A THIRD PERSON, NO KNOWLEDGE OF THEIR MEANING EXCEPT AS A READER, NOT THE REMOTEST PRIVATE RELATION TO THEM.

*Y*et most scholars ignore Kierkegaard's disclaimer for all practical purposes. That is because his slightly twisted shadow falls across every page of the pseudonymous works, and because they are all part of his grandiose plan to deceive his readers into the truth, that is to say to communicate a subjective truth indirectly.

In fact, Kierkegaard's pseudonymous works don't communicate any objective truths at all, not even any concepts. Rather than being knowledge, they are anti-knowledge. This is because knowledge, as Kierkegaard construes it, is always abstract, and existence is always concrete.

KIERKEGAARD STEALS LANGUAGE FROM KNOWLEDGE TO USE IT AGAINST KNOWLEDGE.

As Kierkegaard's wayward disciple Jean-Paul Sartre says,

The Concept of dread BOOM BOOM

Kierkegaard's works are forms of non-knowledge that masquerade as knowledge at the same time that they indict knowledge. Kierkegaard's words self-destruct before our eyes.

They have an Escher-like quality. They lead us nowhere but back into our own selves. Sartre says that Kierkegaard uses objective concepts "regressively, so that the self-destruction of the language necessarily unmasks the one who uses it." For example, the very title of Kierkegaard's book <u>The Concept of Dread</u> is a paradox, for according to him, "dread" (or "anxiety," as another translation has it) is <u>not</u> a concept, rather it is "the non-conceptual foundation of all concepts." (If the first dread, Adam's dread, and the first sin, Adam's sin, are identical, as Kierkegaard holds, and if Adam's sin is that of disobediently eating the fruit of the tree of knowledge, then all knowledge [conceptual thought] is grounded in dread.) Kierkegaard's pseudo-concepts force us away from our own concepts — back into our own freedom, and into our own subjective truths.

As Sartre says, "Reading Kierkegaard, I climb back as far as myself. I want to catch hold of him, and it is myself I catch. This non-conceptual work is an invitation to understand myself as the source of all concepts."

OBJECTIVE
&
SUBJECTIVE
TRUTH

The book in which Kierkegaard develops most clearly the idea of "subjective truth" is <u>Concluding Unscientific Postscript to the Philosophical Fragments</u> (1846), which has become a sort of Bible of existentialism. In this work, written under the pseudonym of "Johannes Climacus," the distinction is drawn between OBJECTIVE and SUBJECTIVE thinking.

To think objectively is to think the universal. Objective thought can only grasp that which can be universalized. A sentence like, "This book is green," is to be analyzed so: We point at an object and categorize it in terms of universal concepts, "Book," and "Greenness." As in Plato's philosophy, to

think the book is to elevate it from the unintelligible world of particulars to the intelligible world of general concepts. The book's particularity cannot be thought, because thinking is always abstracting the general from the particular. Kierkegaard radicalizes Plato. If only that which can be conceptualized can be thought, then "existence" cannot be thought, because it is always concrete and never abstract.

BURP!

Existence is a "surd" which is left over when all analysis is complete. It is the unanalyzable residue which is simply "there." It is, says Kierkegaard, like the frog you discover at the bottom of your beer mug after you have finished your beer. The "concept" of existence is a paradox, which we encounter especially dramatically when we turn to our own existence.

When I am done saying everything that can be said about myself (my name, where I was born, what my ancestry is, what my job is, where I live, how I feel, etc.), there is still something left over — MY EXISTENCE. My existence cannot be thought, and it is not sufficient simply to <u>point</u> at it, as in the case of the green book.

I'M A NUCLEAR ENGINEER. I GRADUATED SUMMA CUM LAUDE. I LIKE TO SKI, READ ROBERT BROWNING, AND BIRD-WATCH. I LIVE IN SAUSALITO IN A TOWNHOUSE WITH A VIEW.

YES, BUT IS ANYBODY EVER HOME?

THE PRESENTATION OF THE SELF AT THE SINGLES BAR

My existence must be lived. It must be existed. But thinking and existing are not the same (even if Descartes did say, "I think, therefore I am"). Existing is a form of DOING, not a form of thinking. Yet it is a form of doing which must be related to thought. (Unthinking action is not Kierkegaard's solution.) The question is, what is the nature of this paradoxical thinking-and-doing which Kierkegaard advocates as his solution to the problem of existence? The kind of thought that is essentially related to doing is what Kierkegaard calls "SUBJECTIVE THOUGHT," and this idea leads to his notorious claim:

TRUTH IS SUBJECTIVITY

Let's examine this.

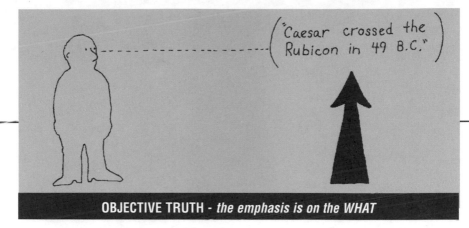

The opposite of subjective truths are objective truths. These are the truths that can be abstracted from reality, conceptualized, and tested—for example, the truths of science, mathematics, and history. In each of these cases there are objective, external criteria to which we appeal when we question the truth of a claim. We can say that individual people are in the truth if what they assert is true. Here, Kierkegaard says, the accent is on the **WHAT**, not on the **HOW**. These truths, however, are existentially indifferent. That is to say, nothing in your life would radically change if you discovered that one of these "truths" was false.

(If new research established that Caesar did not cross the Rubicon in 49 B.C., or that "force" does not equal "mass times acceleration," or even that there is something fishy about the foundations of mathematics, you would not <u>behave</u> much differently, and you certainly wouldn't become a different person.)

WHAT!?

MISSISSIPPI RIVER

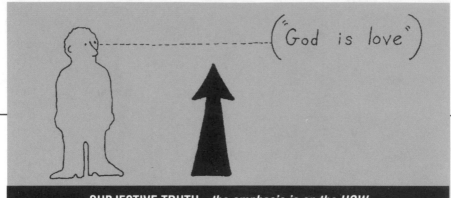

"Subjective truths," on the other hand, are "truths" for which there are no objective criteria to which one can appeal, and yet, for Kierkegaard, they are the most important kind of truths, In their case, the emphasis is on the **HOW** rather than on the **WHAT**. These are existential truths, in that they are essentially related to one's existence, that elusive "surd" which is always <u>there.</u> These truths are not about objective facts, but about values, and about the grounding or foundation of values.

Kierkegaard holds the skeptical view (which he probably got from reading the eighteenth century Scottish philosopher DAVID HUME (1711-1776) that no moral claim can ever be grounded in objective fact. (You can prove that torturing babies causes them pain, but you can't prove that it is morally wrong to torture babies.)

NO "IS" IMPLIES AN "OUGHT"

WHERE EXACTLY IS THE IMMORAL PART?

I'M NOT SURE

Yet Kierkegaard recognized that values, moral, religious, and aesthetic, were essentially related to our idea of selfhood.

ALL DECISIVENESS INHERES IN SUBJECTIVITY

ONLY IN SUBJECTIVITY IS THERE DECISION, TO SEEK OBJECTIVITY IS TO BE IN ERROR

*I*f you truly believe (as opposed to merely <u>saying</u> that you believe) that God is love, or that causing unnecessary misery is wrong, or that beauty must prevail, then these beliefs will be expressed in your actions. (This is what Kierkegaard meant when he said that here the accent is on the <u>how.</u>) And, according to Kierkegaard, if you change your beliefs concerning issues like these, not only will your behavior change, but you will become a different person. In a significant sense, you <u>are </u>your values since your selfhood is the wellspring of your actions. Decision and action are motivated by values, not by facts. No fact by itself can motivate an action. A fact can be the pretext for an action only in the context of values.

As Kierkegaard says:

Yet, in some respects, even facts are determined by values. The facts that reveal themselves to the person motivated by Christian values are different from those that reveal themselves to the person motivated by the value of pleasure, and those that reveal themselves to the political revolutionary are different from those revealed to the conservative. (Think of the famous figure now known as "Wittgenstein's duck/rabbit." My attitude toward the figure is what causes it to reveal itself as a duck rather than as a rabbit.) Kierkegaard would have us recognize that we are the authors of our worlds and have us assume responsibility for that authorship, recognizing that it derives from values that we have chosen. Paradoxically, Kierkegaard refuses to assume responsibility for his authorship of the idea that we must each assume responsibility for our authorship. That is because the idea itself is a subjective truth that cannot be communicated directly. When Kierkegaard liberates the idea from his own authorship and places it in a circle of indirect communication it becomes a possibility that each of us can realize and appropriate for ourselves.

The Duck Rabbit

THERE IS NO SUCH THING AS EXISTENCE WITHOUT RISK.

*I*t follows from all of this that we can never justify the most basic strata of values that make up our lives, hence we can never be certain that we have chosen "the right values." This means, among other things, that there is no such thing as existence without risk, and that existence at its very core must be experienced as anguish or dread by every sensitive soul.

This, then is the grounding of values that concerns subjective thought. The subjective thinker cannot have her own existence as the <u>object</u> of her thought. When something is the object of thought it is abstracted from experience and conceptualized. Only that which has been terminated and is complete can be objectified. But the experience of existence is one of open-endedness and incompleteness. In fact, the experience is as much of something negative as it is of something positive. Kierkegaard says that subjective thought is <u>negative</u> thought. This is because subjective thought ponders the "nothingness that pervades being."

EXPERIENCE IS OPEN-ENDED AND UNFINISHED.

"DEATH"

&
"EXISTENCE"
AS SUBJECTIVE TRUTHS

The phrase "nothingness pervades being" calls attention to the tenuousness and elusiveness of existence. This tenuousness is expressed in the thought of "the possibility of death at any moment."

Kierkegaard's obsession with death seems morbid to some people.

WHAT DID YOU EXPECT FROM A MAN WHOSE LAST NAME MEANS 'CEMETERY!'

But there is some <u>philosophy</u> here and not just psychopathology. That philosophy may be seen in a story that Kierkegaard relates in the <u>Postscript</u>: two men meet on the streets of Copenhagen and one invites the other to dinner. The prospective guest accepts the invitation, saying, "You can count on me quite definitely." As he walks away, a tile blows from the roof and strikes the man dead. Kierkegaard seems to find this story to be hilarious. One could laugh oneself to death over it. But after mocking this man who makes an absolute commitment in the future and who was snuffed from existence by such an insignificant thing as a gust of wind, Kierkegaard concludes that he has been too harsh on the chap.

*S*urely he could not have expected that the fellow respond to the invitation saying: "You can count on me, I shall certainly come; but I must make an exception for the contingency that a tile happens to blow down from a roof and kills me; for in that case I cannot come." But in fact, that is exactly what Kierkegaard expects. If one grasps deeply ("with inwardness," as Kierkegaard calls it) that one can always correctly add to every sentence one utters or thinks the rider, "However, I may be dead in the next moment, in which case I cannot attend," then one has discovered one's death as a subjective truth, and one is in a position to order one's priorities accordingly.

Perhaps it will no longer seem so important that one's socks be without holes, or that one's shirt matches one's jacket. This individual will be able to make decisions that are the result of concentrating attention on human existence as it is lived, neither in the past nor in the distant future, but in the now. Kierkegaard's goal is not to cause us to shiver in terror at the discovery of the tenuousness of existence, rather he hopes that by facilitating the discovery of our death as subjective truth, he can help us to discover our lives.

43

It is actually possible to live one's whole life outside oneself, it is possible to live purely in terms of ritualized formats and social roles, and never come in contact with the truth of one's own subjectivity. But Kierkegaard does everything possible to prevent that tragedy, the tragedy of the man "who woke up one day and discovered he was dead."

WHAT A SHAME TO HAVE DIED BEFORE ONE LIVED.

Much of the existentialist literature influenced by Kierkegaard's philosophy also concentrates on the discovery of existence as a subjective truth. Merseault, the protagonist of Albert Camus's (1913-1960) novel, <u>The Stranger</u>, has never truly lived a day of his life, yet he finally discovers his life in the shadow of the guillotine. The night before his execution for a murder he cannot recall committing, Merseault violently throws a priest out of his prison cell. This is the first human act he has ever performed. He goes to the barred window and smells roses in the air. He has never smelled roses before. He sees the moon over the frame of the guillotine, and he stares at it. He had never <u>looked</u> at the moon before. Suddenly, and for the first time, he lives. The fact that he will die tomorrow does not matter. He <u>has</u> lived. Not everyone can say as much.

A similar message is communicated in Ingmar Bergman's very Kierkegaardian film, "The Seventh Seal." Antonius Bloch, the disillusioned knight, returning from the crusades to his plague-ravaged homeland, sends his squire to ask directions of a man sleeping on the beach. The squire tries rudely to awaken the man, pulling back his cape from his head, and finds himself staring into the gaping jaws of an eyeless skull. When the squire returns to his master, the knight asks, "Did he speak?" The squire responds, "Most eloquently!" This is a very Kierkegaardian message.

In another scene in the same film the knight, who is playing chess with Death, goes into a church and reveals to the confessor his strategy for defeating his adversary. The robed confessor pulls back his hood, revealing himself as Death, and he thanks the stunned knight for the revelation. Antonius Bloch, who now knows for certain he will die, grabs the bars of the priest's cell. He stares in horror at his own clenched fist, then slowly begins to notice the veins and muscles in his taut wrist, and says out loud to himself, "This is my hand, I can move it, feel the blood pulsing through it. The sun is still high in the sky, and I, Antonius Bloch, am playing chess with Death." Again, this is the Kierkegaardian message. The positive—existence—can only be understood by an acute awareness of the negative— the "nothingness which pervades existence."

*S*o, according to Kierkegaard, these kinds of existential insights, along with moral and religious values, are "subjective truths" in that there are no objective criteria to establish their validity, and, to be made valid, they must be appropriated by the individual, internalized, and reflected in one's decisions and actions. Subjective truths are not pieces of knowledge, rather they are ways of arranging knowledge and activating it. These "truths" are grounded not in some facts about the external world, but in the discovery of the evasiveness, the tenuousness, and the uncertainty of life, that is to say, in the nothingness of existence. This discovery must be made by each individual for herself or himself alone. Kierkegaard's pseudonymous authorship, with its "indirect communication," is meant to facilitate this discovery. Kierkegaard calls it "deceiving his reader into the truth."

APPARENTLY THE EXISTENTIAL INSIGHT CAN COME TO ONE LIKE A BOLT FROM THE BLUE.

At one point in his book Either/Or, Kierkegaard's pseudonymous writer says to his reader, if you reach the point that is the moment of decision,

THROW THIS BOOK DOWN!

Consciousness is the Problem

The discussion of subjective and objective truths may have left the impression that only subjective truths are philosophically problematical for Kierkegaard, while objective truths are straightforward. But we see that even so-called objective truths are fraught with problems when we turn to Kierkegaard's treatment of the famous quest for certainty of **RENE' DESCARTES.** Descartes (1596-1650), the father of modern philosophy, found that claims of knowledge about the external world were unreliable unless they could be grounded upon some absolutely certain foundation. Using a method of doubt summarized in the motto, "de omnibus dubitandum est" ("everything is to be doubted"), Descartes concluded that everything could be doubted <u>except</u> consciousness.

It seems to me....

that I see a dog.

His famous dictum, perhaps the most famous in Western philosophy, "I THINK, THEREFORE I AM," is the proclamation of the absolute certainty discovered in one's own consciousness.

Everything else is suspicious.

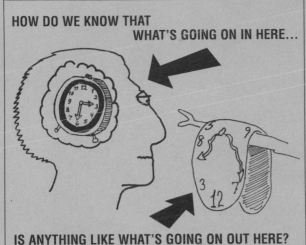

HOW DO WE KNOW THAT WHAT'S GOING ON IN HERE...

IS ANYTHING LIKE WHAT'S GOING ON OUT HERE?

You can't trust the information brought in through the senses, because "the senses are known deceivers."

You can't trust common sense—our ordinary way of thinking about the world—because it is impossible to prove for certain at any particular moment that you are not dreaming instead of being in a waking state.

I'M WIDE AWAKE

CARTESIAN DREAMS

$$X = (2Y - [\tfrac{1}{2}Y \times 4]) + [20 \div 5] - [16^2 + 2]$$

DIVIDED BY ITSELF AND FLUSHED DOWN THE TOILET

HEH HEH HEH HEH

THE EVIL GENIE INVENTS MATH

You can't trust math, because you can't prove that reality as you conceive it has not been constructed by an all-powerful "evil genie" as a system of undetectable mathematical errors.

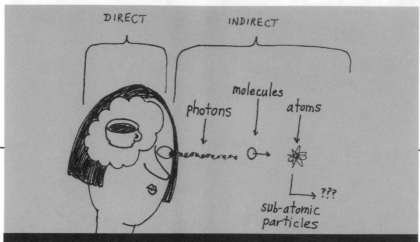

DIRECT   INDIRECT

photons   molecules   atoms

sub-atomic particles   ???

WE ARE IN DIRECT CONTACT WITH THE CONTENTS OF OUR OWN MINDS, AND IN INDIRECT CONTACT WITH THE CONTENTS OF THE EXTERNAL WORLD.

But the one thing you can trust, according to Descartes, is the certainty of your own consciousness, because every time you say to yourself, "I THINK" (or "I am thinking"), you are <u>right</u>—even if the senses deceive, even if you are in a dream state, even if you are in a world created by a malevolent demon. The very effort to doubt the proposition ends up proving it, because

"doubting" is a form of "thinking." What makes consciousness certain for Descartes is its immediacy. It present itself DIRECTLY to the thinking subject. It does not pass through any <u>medium</u> that might contaminate or falsify it. Not even an evil genius could get between the subject and her consciousness. So any sentence that does nothing but <u>express</u> consciousness as it is experienced is necessarily true.

EVEN IF I AM DECEIVED BY YOU IN EVERY OTHER WAY, IF I THINK "I AM," THEN I AM

DAMN! HE AM.

Such a sentence is,
"I THINK, THEREFORE I AM."

God

innate ideas

mathematical physics

THE CIRCUITOUS ROUTE TO THE EXTERNAL WORLD

Upon the certainty of consciousness and selfhood (which are identical for Descartes), he is able to build a complicated deductive system that allows him to conclude finally that objective truths about the external world can be found in the science of mathematical physics (of the type that he, Galileo, and in the next generation Isaac Newton practiced.)

But Descartes would be quick to admit that scientific knowledge of the world is only as good as the foundation on which it rests, namely, the certainty of consciousness. But at least this foundation was unassailable, Descartes believed, as did most philosophers for the next 200 years.

Nevertheless, Kierkegaard assails it, in a book ironically titled, <u>De Omnibus Dubitandum Est</u> (1842-43) written pseudonymously, once again under the name of Johannes Climacus.

A STRUCTURE IS ONLY AS GOOD AS ITS FOUNDATION.

We have seen that Descartes believed himself to have overcome doubt by discovering the immediacy and certainty of consciousness. "Johannes Climacus" argued that there is neither immediacy nor certainty in consciousness. Johannes says:

> THAT'S JOHANNES CLIMACUS

> THAT'S ODD. IT LOOKS LIKE SØREN KIERKEGAARD WITH A FAKE NOSE AND MOUSTACHE

> Cannot consciousness then remain in immediacy?...If a man could not speak, then he would remain in immediacy.... Immediacy is actuality. Speech is ideality. Consciousness is opposition or contradiction. The moment I express reality the opposition is there. The possibility of doubt then lies in consciousness, whose very essence is to be a kind of contradiction or opposition. It is produced by, and itself produces, duplicity.

WORD. POSSIBILITY. IDEALITY. WHAT IS NOT. ABSTRACT.

SENSATION. ACTUALITY. REALITY. WHAT IS. CONCRETE.

CONSCIOUSNESS

CONCIOUSNESS HOLDS TOGETHER SETS OF CONTRADICTIONS

What does this complicated assertion mean? It means that there could be immediacy and certainty in sensation, but this immediate certainty would disappear as soon as the experience is expressed in thought or language. For thought and language are not the same as reality. They are opposed to reality. They are reality's "other." To think of something or to name it is to oppose it with otherness. In consciousness, that which is (actuality) is confronted by that which is not (possibility). To think, "this is a door," is to be conscious of it as something that could be open, or that could be locked, or could imprison me. It is something that was open, is not now open, but that will be open later.

So consciousness is the collision between actuality and possibility, between what is and what is not. Consciousness is then a form of opposition, of "doubleness." Kierkegaard points out that the word "doubt" is also etymologically related to doubleness. (This is true in both Danish and English.) He concludes that consciousness, far from being a form of certainty, is a form of uncertainty. Far from overcoming doubt, as Descartes believed, consciousness <u>is</u> a form of doubt, because in consciousness, that which <u>is</u> is in question — <u>de omnibus dubitandum est</u>.

What Kierkegaard is stressing here is the uncertainty of all thought—uncertain because unstable. What the old Greek philosopher HERACLITUS (c. 470 B.C.) believed to be true of the world—that it was in a constant state of flux, that "you can't step in the same river twice"—Kierkegaard believes to be true of consciousness.

We can fail to know this only by <u>choosing</u> not to know it, by being in a state of what Jean-Paul Sartre calls "bad faith." The reason for choosing not to know it is clear enough. It is because there is a kind of <u>terror</u> in consciousness. Sartre has been most impressed with this aspect of Kierkegaard's theory of consciousness.

HERACLITUS: YOU CAN'T STEP IN THE SAME RIVER TWICE

Sartre says that consciousness is "an impersonal, monstrous spontaneity... a vertigo of possibility," and he adds, "consciousness is terrified by its own spontaneity." He goes on to say that for the person who does not deceive himself or herself in this respect, all the guardrails of social certainty and stability collapse. Kierkegaard and Sartre see the complacent, self-satisfied bourgeois inhabitant of Copenhagen and Paris, respectively, as living a kind of inauthentic life.

Kierkegaard's analysis ultimately leads him to justify a certain kind of religious thought, an option that Sartre thinks is no longer open to us. Kierkegaard's argument runs something like this: The <u>negative</u> is present in all consciousness. <u>Doubt</u> accentuates the negative, <u>Belief</u> chooses to cancel the negative. Every mental act is composed of doubt and belief, but it is belief that is the positive, it is belief that sustains thought and holds the world together. Nevertheless, belief understands itself as uncertain, as not justified by any objective fact.

ANGUISH

A person sustains the relationship between consciousness and the world through an act of belief. A complete failure of belief, that is, the maximizing of doubt, would lead to the kind of madness that is the consequence of Descartes' radical doubt (<u>De omnibus dubitandum</u>…) taken to its logical extreme.

> I'M NOT SURE IF THERE'S AN EXTERNAL WORLD. I CAN'T TELL IF I'M DREAMING. MAYBE THERE'S AN EVIL GENIE.

> SANTA CLAUS? EASTER BUNNY? TOOTH-FAIRY? EXTERNAL WORLD?

So, for Kierkegaard, "objective truths" about the world are grounded in belief, not in certainty. That belief can be a naive, unquestioning, childlike pre-philosophical belief, but at some point Kierkegaard seems to feel, everyone comes to suspect his or her naiveté—that is to say, begins to philosophize. Then there are only two possibilities. Either one flees into bad faith (that is, <u>pretends</u> not to suspect) or one comes to the realization that normal states of consciousness are more like religious states of consciousness than we had realized, in that, rather than being states of certainty, both are composed of a strange mixture of doubt and belief.

> I BELIEVE IN THE FATHER, THE SON, AND THE HOLY GHOST

> I BELIEVE IN THE TABLE, THE CHAIR, AND THE COFFEE CUP

The religious paradox, of the would-be disciple who said to Jesus, "Master, I believe. Help thou me in mine unbelief," now becomes a paradox of everyday consciousness. It is the recognition of this paradox in the Kierkegaardian account of consciousness that subverts the smooth, comfortable smugness of everyday life, revealing a hidden kind of terror, not just in the world, but in consciousness itself. It gives centrality to the experience of "the collapsing of the guardrails," as Sartre calls it, or of what Freud calls "the psychopathology of everyday life." It is perhaps best expressed in the fiction of Franz Kafka, particularly in his story of "K.," the man who could become a cockroach, and who did. There is a madness at the heart of normality. Only belief can overcome the madness and the doubt. Yet even belief, taken to its extreme form—religious belief—is itself a form of madness and doubt, but one which literally has, for Kierkegaard, a saving grace.

YE GODS! I COULD TURN INTO A HUMAN BEING!

DREAD

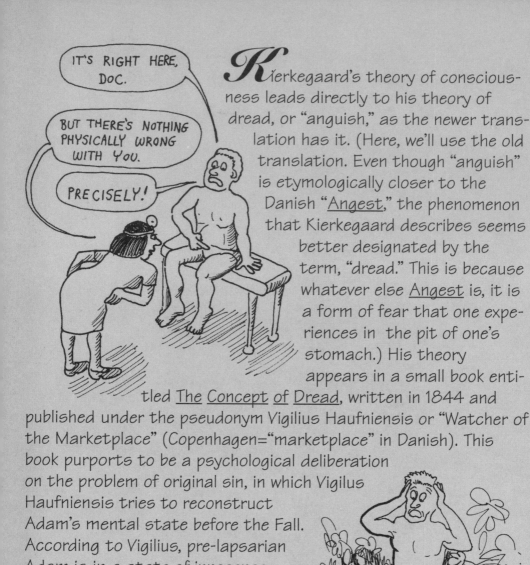

IT'S RIGHT HERE, DOC.

BUT THERE'S NOTHING PHYSICALLY WRONG WITH YOU.

PRECISELY!

Kierkegaard's theory of consciousness leads directly to his theory of dread, or "anguish," as the newer translation has it. (Here, we'll use the old translation. Even though "anguish" is etymologically closer to the Danish "Angest," the phenomenon that Kierkegaard describes seems better designated by the term, "dread." This is because whatever else Angest is, it is a form of fear that one experiences in the pit of one's stomach.) His theory appears in a small book entitled The Concept of Dread, written in 1844 and published under the pseudonym Vigilius Haufniensis or "Watcher of the Marketplace" (Copenhagen="marketplace" in Danish). This book purports to be a psychological deliberation on the problem of original sin, in which Vigilus Haufniensis tries to reconstruct Adam's mental state before the Fall. According to Vigilius, pre-lapsarian Adam is in a state of innocence, which is a state of peace and repose, but he is also in a state of dread. What is the object of Adam's dread? It is nothing. It is no thing. It is his own freedom that Adam dreads, for Adam dreads possibility. He dreads that which is not, but which may be. He dreads what he may do, what he is free to do.

When God pronounces the prohibition against eating the fruit of the tree of knowledge, this prohibition induces a state of dread in Adam "because the prohibition awakens in him the possibility of freedom." Kierkegaard defines dread as freedom's appearance before itself as "possibility." But freedom, according to Kierkegaard, is never only possible. As soon as it is suspected, it is actual. Dread, then, is the fear of freedom. Says Vigilius, "However deep the individual has sunk, he may sink still deeper, and this <u>may</u> is the object of dread."

$\mathcal{W}$e have all experienced the phenomenon that Kierkegaard talks of here; sometimes we experience it as pathology. Driving along a narrow road on a rainy night, annoyed at an oncoming car's bright headlights, the thought flits through one's mind, " I _could_ drive right into him." This "I COULD" is freedom, and it is the object of dread. One fears the monstrousness of freedom. There is <u>nothing</u> to prevent me from driving into him, nothing but <u>myself</u>. Or, as Sartre says, while walking along a steep mountain path, we may fear slipping on loose ground and falling into the chasm, but we also fear <u>throwing</u> ourselves into it. This fear is dread. This is right in line with Kierkegaard's point, who says: "One may liken dread to dizziness. He whose eye chances to look down into the yawning abyss becomes dizzy." The yawning abyss here is one's own freedom.

We must add to all this Kierkegaard's more technical definition of dread:

That is, dread is the desire for what one fears and the fear of what one desires. Once Adam knows he <u>can</u> disobey God, he desires to do so, and he dreads his own desire, because he knows that as a free being there is nothing but himself to stop him from sinning.

Furthermore, Kierkegaard tells us that consciousness of the future expresses itself as dread. This reveals another sense in which the object of dread is nothing. The future does not exist. It is nothing. And yet, unlike the past, which is solid and unchangeable, the future, <u>my</u> future, must still be created, by me, in my freedom. I create my future through my every choice and decision. I must even create <u>myself</u> in the future. As Sartre says, "I await myself in the future. Anguish is the fear of not finding myself there." Dread is the fear of the awesome responsibility of self-creation. It is a fear of freedom. The alternative of dread is not inno- cence, for there was dread even in innocence. The alternative

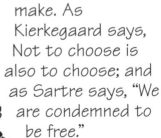

is inauthenticity, Sartre's "bad faith," a flight from freedom, a choosing not to be free. But of course, this is the one choice we cannot make. As Kierkegaard says, Not to choose is also to choose; and as Sartre says, "We are condemned to be free."

DESPAIR

$\mathcal{W}$e've talked about dread and anguish. Now we must look at another bleak topic—DESPAIR. Just as Kierkegaard's obsession with death seems morbid to many of his readers, so do the very titles of some of his books seem loaded with negativity—books with names like <u>Fear</u> <u>and</u> <u>Trembling</u>, <u>The</u> <u>Concept</u> <u>of</u> <u>Dread</u>, and <u>The</u> <u>Sickness</u> <u>unto</u> <u>Death</u>. It is quite definitely the case that Kierkegaard concentrated on the dark side of human experience, but he had his reasons, some of which may have to do with person-al pathology, but some of which were deeply philosophical.

Kierkegaard's obsession with abnormal states of consciousness derive from his view that so-called "normality" disguises the true significance of what it means to BE, and that when one has been pushed to the very edge of existence, one has a perspective providing a deeper insight into human reality. With this notion in mind, we turn now to some of Kierkegaard's ideas in his The Sickness unto Death (1849). He begins the book with a tremendously complicated paragraph:

THIS...IS...ABSURD

MAN IS SPIRIT. BUT WHAT IS SPIRIT? SPIRIT IS THE SELF. BUT WHAT IS THE SELF? THE SELF IS A RELATION WHICH RELATES ITSELF TO ITS OWN SELF.... MAN IS A SYNTHESIS OF THE INFINITE AND THE FINITE, OF THE TEMPORAL AND THE ETERNAL, OF POSSIBILITY AND NECESSITY, IN SHORT, IT IS A SYNTHESIS. A SYNTHESIS IS A RELATION BETWEEN TWO FACTORS. SO REGARDED, MAN IS NOT YET A SELF.

Was Kierkegaard joking here, as Woody Allen seems to suggest in his comment on this passage?

THE CONCEPT BROUGHT TEARS TO MY EYES. MY WORD, I THOUGHT, TO BE THAT CLEVER! (I'M A MAN WHO HAS TROUBLE WRITING TWO MEANINGFUL SENTENCES ON "MY DAY AT THE ZOO.") TRUE, THE PASSAGE WAS TOTALLY INCOMPREHENSIBLE TO ME, BUT WHAT OF IT AS LONG AS KIERKEGAARD WAS HAVING FUN?

Perhaps. But Kierkegaard's jokes are philosophical jokes meant to be taken seriously. Let us plunge into this joke's murky depths.

We find that the self (or "spir- it") is the <u>act</u> of relating two opposing poles, which can oversimply be called "body" and "soul." This act is not one that takes place automati- cally once and for all, rather it must be constantly performed if selfhood is to be maintained. The attempt to establish the syn- thesis is like Aristotle's attempt to achieve "the golden mean" in moral action. One can err by being too much attract- ed to the idea of body-as-self.

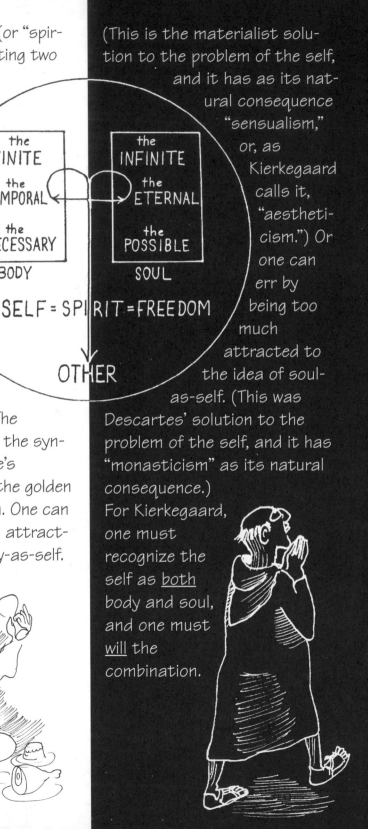

the FINITE
the TEMPORAL
the NECESSARY
BODY

the INFINITE
the ETERNAL
the POSSIBLE
SOUL

SELF = SPIRIT = FREEDOM

OTHER

(This is the materialist solu- tion to the problem of the self, and it has as its nat- ural consequence "sensualism," or, as Kierkegaard calls it, "aestheti- cism.") Or one can err by being too much attracted to the idea of soul- as-self. (This was Descartes' solution to the problem of the self, and it has "monasticism" as its natural consequence.) For Kierkegaard, one must recognize the self as <u>both</u> body and soul, and one must <u>will</u> the combination.

Kierkegaard now adds to his already complicated definition of the self:

> Such a derived, constituted relation is the human self, a relation which relates itself to its own self, and in relating itself to its own self relates itself to another.

So we see that there are two relationships to be sustained: one between body and soul, and one between the self and "another." Kierkegaard is clearly basing his thoughts on the famous analysis of the self put forth by G.W.F. HEGEL (1760-1831), a philosopher who both deeply influenced Kierkegaard and deeply offended him. (In fact the "joke" in Kierkegaard's definition of the self that we looked at is a joke on Hegel, for Kierkegaard is parodying Hegel's abstruse and paradoxical language.) In a chapter of his Phenomenology of Spirit (1807) called "Lordship and Bondage," Hegel had said,

I LOVE HIM. NO... I HATE HIM

"Self-consciousness exists in itself and for itself, in that, and by the fact that it exists for another self-consciousness." For Hegel, the self exists only by virtue of being recognized by the Other. The lord exists as lord only because he is seen as such by the bondsman and the bondsman becomes bondsman because he is seen as such by the lord, so they each constitute each other's being.

For Hegel, this fact sets up a complicated dialectical system of mutual dependence and antagonism between the two.

Kierkegaard also sees the self as constituted by the Other. There is one form of selfhood—the religious self—that is constituted by a commitment to God, and another form of selfhood—the ethical self—which is constituted by a commitment to humanity, or to a specific human being.

(For Kierkegaard, <u>marriage</u> would be just such a defining relationship to the ethical. He could have consecrated himself to Regina Olsen, thereby establishing an ethical self. Instead he consecrated himself to God.)

The achievement of a Kierkegaardian selfhood is even more complicated than it has been described here, involving as it does choosing one self in one's historical, cultural, and geographical condition, with one's own genetic endowment (without conceiving oneself as a mere <u>product</u> of these conditions—that is, as a <u>victim</u> of them). No surprise that most people despair of achieving true selfhood. <u>The Sickness unto Death</u> is mainly about the many forms that despair takes on. We will briefly inspect a few of these forms.

Despair is the opposite of "willing to be that self which one truly is." This is what he calls "the sickness unto death." It is not that despair leads to bodily death, rather despair <u>longs</u> for death.

The person who despairs, despairs of becoming the self he (potentially) is, so he wishes to become nothing. He despairs "because he cannot consume himself, cannot get rid of himself, cannot become nothing." Therefore, he is consumed by a death-wish, but usually this death-wish is unconscious. There are degrees of despair running the gamut from unconscious despair to the most acute consciousness of despair. And,

Kierkegaard says, "the more consciousness, the more intense the despair." But the good news is, the more intense the despair, the closer at hand is the solution.

UNCONSCIOUS DESPAIR

CONSCIOUS DESPAIR

Unconscious despair is one in which the individual identifies herself with something outside herself, therefore her destiny as a self is controlled by a whim of fate.

thus when the ambitious man whose watchword was "Either Caesar or nothing" does not become Caesar, he is in despair thereat,... precisely because he did not become Caesar he now cannot endure to be himself... what is intolerable to him is that he cannot get rid of himself.

This form of despair produces an emptiness. "There is a blind door in the background of his soul, behind which there is nothing."

72   **DESPAIR AT THE COSTUME PARTY**

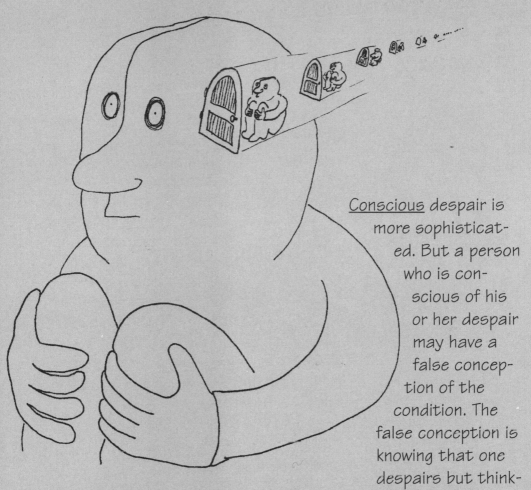

Conscious despair is more sophisticated. But a person who is conscious of his or her despair may have a false conception of the condition. The false conception is knowing that one despairs but thinking that others do not (and despairing over that fact as well.) The true conception is knowing that despair is a human condition and recognizing oneself in that condition.

Conscious despair incorrectly conceived is the despair of introversion. In this case, behind the blind door "sits as it were the self and watches itself employed in filling up time with not willing to be itself." This form of despair may be that of a Hamlet, who, incapable of action, hires actors to perform the action that he himself should perform.

This allusion becomes even more pertinent when we realize that, according to Kierkegaard, the biggest danger here is that of suicide. Here the unconscious death-wish becomes conscious. But the possibility of survival is found in the fact that the despair begins to become <u>passionate</u>, and where there is passion, there is the will to live. If the individual passes through the suicidal crisis, if he has rejected suicide, he has willed existence. Whose existence? His own. He wills himself, but he does not believe his self-realization is possible, so he despairs.

THESE THINGS ARE TRUE OF ME, SO THEY MUST BE TRUE OF YOU.

IF YOU HAVEN'T HAD THESE ABNORMAL EXPERIENCES, THERE MUST BE SOMETHING WRONG WITH YOU.

(The masculine pronoun "he" is being used here because this is all clearly Kierkegaardian autobiography. He has passed through these stages of despair, and he generalizes from his case to that of the whole human race.)

This form of despair merges into the next and last form, which Kierkegaard calls the despair of <u>defiance.</u> Now rather than being resigned to his despair, the individual is offended by it. His passion turns into a demonic rage. He <u>becomes</u> his torment and his fury. His selfhood passionately crystallizes around them. At last he has a self that he has willed, but it is a "demonic self." In his rage, he becomes the

I'M NOT GOING TO TAKE IT ANYMORE!

fight against the offending forces. But this is a fight that in fact he does not want to win. "He rages most of all at the thought that eternity might get it into its head to take his misery from him." This is a battle he cannot afford to win, because he <u>is</u> the battle against the forces of alienation. If he wins his battle, he loses his self. He is no one.

THIS IS <u>MY</u> MISERY. YOU'D BETTER NOT TRY TO TAKE IT AWAY FROM ME!

But this demonical self in its rage has been driven close to the precipice, therefore close to the possibility of what Kierkegaard calls "the leap"—a leap into true selfhood. To witness the actualization of this possibility, we must study Kierkegaard's conception of the three kinds of selfhood.

THE THREE SPHERES OF EXISTENCE

Kierkegaard divides humanity into three possible modes of existence:

"the aesthetical,"

"the ethical,"

and "the religious."

Each of these modes of existence is more than just a "stage on life's way," as he sometimes calls them, rather they are whole human worlds, complete with their own ideals, motivations, and forms of behavior. Each one is a complete world view. Any one of these frames of reference can be chosen voluntarily by the individual, but one of them, the aesthetic, is more basic than the others in that even those who never make any conscious choice concerning their fundamental stance in the world find themselves in "aestheticism" along with those who have consciously chosen it.

THE
AESTHETIC
SPHERE

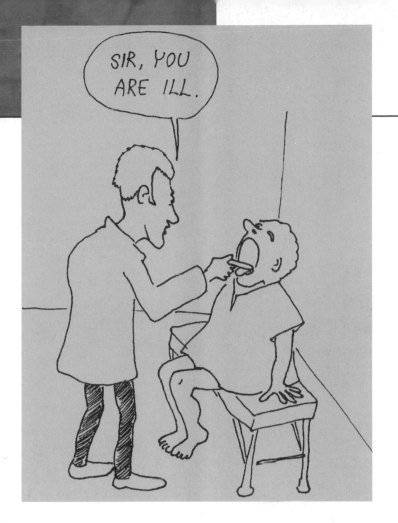

Because Kierkegaard believed that aestheticism could not really provide a true form of selfhood, rather it was a form of ALIENATION from selfhood, he spent a great deal of time describing it, diagnosing it, and prescribing medicaments for it. These analyses of the aesthetic realm are carried out by Kierkegaard's pseudonymous personae, most of whom are themselves aesthetes. (Obviously this is an aspect of Kierkegaard's method of ironic indirect communication.) Some of these aesthetes are well aware of their own plight, while others are only capable of great insight into the weakness of their fellows, but blind to their own failings.

Just as the aesthetic realm represents a step in a hierarchy, it is itself hierarchical, with the most sophisticated (hence sickest) aesthete at the top of the scale. The lowest rungs are occupied by the completely uncouth—in today's world perhaps the "couchpotato" sitting in his undershirt with a can of beer in hand in front of the television watching his second Sunday afternoon football game. Neither Kierkegaard's sophisticated aesthetes nor Kiekegaard himself have anything but disdain for this fellow.

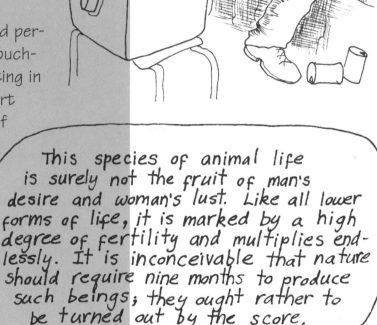

This species of animal life is surely not the fruit of man's desire and woman's lust. Like all lower forms of life, it is marked by a high degree of fertility and multiplies endlessly. It is inconceivable that nature should require nine months to produce such beings; they ought rather to be turned out by the score.

A bit higher up on the scale are those who inhabit the business world. (They are "aesthetes" because their idea of "the good" is the pleasure produced while engaging in a clever business deal.) But they hardly fare better in the estimation of the pseudonymous writers, one of whom says:

OF ALL RIDICULOUS THINGS, IT SEEMS TO ME THE MOST RIDICULOUS IS TO BE A BUSY MAN OF AFFAIRS, PROMPT TO MEALS AND PROMPT TO WORK. HENCE WHEN I SEE A FLY SETTLE DOWN IN A CRUCIAL MOMENT ON THE NOSE OF A BUSINESS MAN, OR SEE HIM BESPATTERED BY A CARRIAGE WHICH PASSES BY HIM IN EVEN GREATER HASTE, OR A DRAWBRIDGE OPENS BEFORE HIM, OR A TILE FROM THE ROOF FALLS DOWN AND STRIKES HIM DEAD, THEN I LAUGH HEARTILY.

(Kierkegaard has a thing about falling tiles!)

Finally, there are the aristocratic hedonists whose cultivation of aestheticism sets them off as being high above the other groups. By far the greatest part of Kierkegaard's analysis of the aesthetic realm focuses on the top rungs of the hierarchical ladder. There are several reasons for this.

First, his natural elitism prevents him from making a sympathetic scrutiny of the unsophisticated.

Furthermore, he correctly realized that the unsophisticated were not his audience. He would not be read by them.

Third, most of Kierkegaard's insights are drawn from self-analysis, and he was well aware that he was in imminent danger of losing himself to the temptations of refined aestheticism. Hence, his work in this field is not just descriptive, but confessional and of great urgency to Kierkegaard personally.

What all forms of aestheticism have in common, from the most boorish to the most refined manifestations, is that they are governed by what Freud would later call "the pleasure principle," the pursuit of pleasure and the flight from pain.

I CALL IT THAT BECAUSE THAT'S WHAT IT IS

Hence, "aestheticism" is a form of hedonism.

People who find themselves in the aesthetic realm have their lives governed by the principles of sensuousness. This is so whether one's idea of fun is stuffing oneself with chocolate donuts and getting drunk on cheap wine, beating a business competitor out of an account, or discussing a fine point of a Shakespearean sonnet.

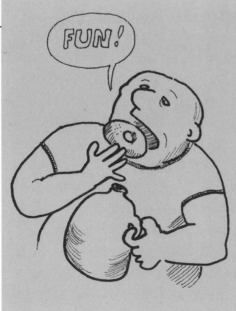

FUN!

The result of being guided by the pleasure principle, whether consciously or unconsciously and whether in its crude or refined form, is that one is never in control of one's self. The aesthete's life is governed by external contingencies and arbitrariness.

Furthermore, aesthetes never achieve a truly <u>human</u> form of existence, because they are guided by the same principles that motivate amoebas and slugs. Pleasure and pain are, after all, fundamentally biological in nature. It is true that the more refined is the pleasure, the more "spiritual" it seems to become, but for Kierkegaard, this spirituality is only an illusion. In fact, the evolution of the aesthete from crassness to sophistication is based on the realization that pleasure must be transformed into a form of <u>consciousness</u> rather than remain mere physical titillation. The sophisticated aesthete realizes that the pursuit of pleasure itself becomes boring, but he ("he" because Kierkegaard's aesthetes are always male) tries to solve this problem from <u>within</u> the aesthetic sphere. He does so by creating a world of exotic bohemian sensuality of the spirit. The aesthete does not yet recognize that boredom is actually a manifestation of despair.

One of Kierkegaard's anonymous aesthetes makes the following observation:

"Boredom is the root of all evil. The history of this can be traced from the very beginning of the world. The gods were bored, so they created man. Adam was bored because he was alone, and so Eve was created. Thus boredom entered the world and increased in proportion to the increase in population. Adam was bored alone; then Adam and Eve were bored together; then Adam and Eve and Cain and Abel were bored en famille; then the population of the world increased, and the peoples were bored en masse. To divert themselves they conceived the idea of constructing a tower high enough to reach the heavens. This idea is itself as boring as the tower was high and constitutes a terrible proof of how boredom gained the upper hand."

ISN'T THERE ANYTHING TO DO?

NO

NO

NO

Kierkegaard's sophisticated aesthete concludes:

There are the unsophisticated bores ("the mob, the crowd") who bore others. And there are the sophisticated bores ("the elect, the aristocracy") who bore themselves. The sophisticated form of boredom has DEATH as its natural consequence: these aristocratic aesthetes "either die of boredom (the passive form) or shoot themselves out of curiosity (the active form)."

ALL MEN ARE BORES...

ROTATE YOUR PLEASURES

GENTLEMAN FARMER

CIGARS

COGNAC

THE NAKED BODY

To avoid the boredom to which the pursuit of pleasure usually leads, the aesthetic author of the above passage prescribes what he calls "the Rotation Method." This method will allow you to create your own world of pleasure. To do so, you must avoid friendship, love, marriage, business, commitments of any sort, and intense pleasures and pains. You perform certain acts that allow you to create your own unpredicted pleasures.

You badger sentimental people, you fall in love— not with a woman, but with the <u>idea</u> of a woman—that way, if she dies, you won't be affected. (In fact, you'll be better off!) "You go to see the middle of a play, you read the third part of a book." You remain outside of life, a spectator and a manipulator. This way you will rescue freedom from necessity and fill your life with cunning little surprises that, with good luck, will keep you from being swamped by life's tedium.

Nevertheless, the more frenzied is the pursuit of the rotation method, the more despairing the aesthete becomes, and the closer he comes to suicide. In his journal entries we discover a bitter cynicism, a world-weariness:

"There are well-known insects that die in the moment of fecundation. So it is with all joy; life's supreme and richest moment of pleasure is coupled with death."

Here we see that Kierkegaard links sexual pleasure, the most extreme and sought-after pleasure, with death. Like Freud, seventy-five years later, Kierkegaard seems to have discovered that the secret of the pleasure principle is a death wish. This discovery constitutes an absolute indictment of aestheticism.

If one lingers in the aesthetic sphere after having seen the pleasure principle for what it is, cynical apathy can be the only result. Kierkegaard's jaded hedonist writes:

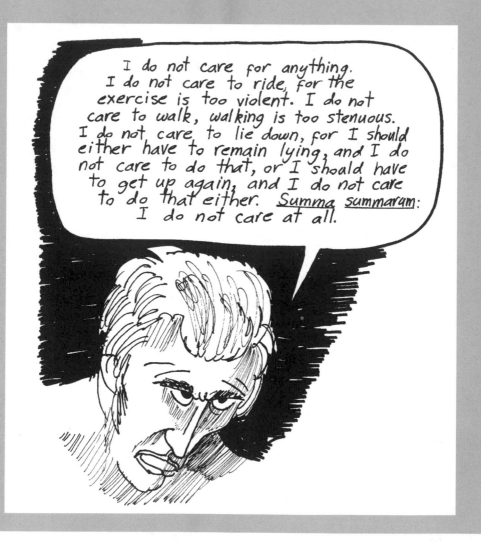

...and

The last line of this "ecstatic lecture," as Kierkegaard calls it, reveals another layer of meaning behind his skirmish with the aesthetic mentality.

Perhaps the conclusion of the "lecture" is not the sum and substance of <u>all</u> philosophy, but for Kierkegaard it is the sum and substance of all <u>Hegelian</u> philosophy. We have already mentioned that the metaphysics of George Wilhelm Friedrich Hegel had deeply influenced Kierkegaard. Hegel had the uncanny knack of evoking hostile attacks from those whom he most influenced. This is particularly true of his most famous "disciples," Karl Marx and Søren Kierkegaard. The very titles of some of Kierkegaard's works are parodies of Hegel, who, upon completing his theories, believed that most all philosophical problems had been solved by what he called his "System." He did, however, admit that there might be a few loose ends which needed to be tied together, but he supposed that such could be a accomplished in a short postscript to his System that would be written by his disciples.

In response, Kierkegaard writes his <u>Philosophical Fragments,</u> which, rather than being systematic philosophy in the Hegelian style, is fragmentary philosophy; then he writes a postscript to the <u>Fragments</u> that is exactly four times longer than the book to which it is a postscript. This book, as we have seen, he titles <u>Concluding Unscientific Postscript</u>. The implication concerning the "short, systematic postscript" to Hegel's philosophy is obvious.

Similarly, Kierkegaard's book <u>Either/Or</u> parodies Hegel's philosophy. Hegel had claimed to have discovered an error in the traditional logic that had been set forth in the third century B.C. by Aristotle. According to Hegel, Aristotle's LAW OF IDENTITY (A=A), his LAW OF NON-CONTRADICTION (not both A and not-A) and the LAW OF THE EXCLUDED MIDDLE (either A or not-A) had all misconstrued reality. The implication of these laws, Hegel said, was that everything in reality was static and black and white. To the contrary, according to him, reality was in flux and consisted of constantly changing hues of gray. Hegel wanted to replace traditional Aristotelian logic with a new dialectical logic according to which the traditional laws of logic were subverted. The Principle of Identity was wrong because everything was always <u>more</u> than itself. The Principle of Non-Contradiction was wrong because everything is both itself and <u>not</u> itself. The Principle of the Excluded Middle was also wrong; Hegel replaces the "either/or" with a "both/and," thereby allowing a multiplicity of possibilities that were excluded by Aristotelian logic.

Now Kierkegaard was at least as aware as Hegel of the Heraclitian nature of reality and thought. Nevertheless, he believed that Hegel had made a profound error when he abolished the principles of logic, and particularly the Law of the Excluded Middle, for not only had Hegel dissolved all distinctions and thereby turned his metaphysics into that "night in which all cows are black," but he had also removed the possibility of decisiveness, and thereby, of freedom. That is to say, Hegel had declared war on that which is human, subjectivity. If there is no "either/or," then there is nothing human. Therefore Kierkegaard titles the book in which he discusses all this Either/Or, implying thereby that Hegel himself was deeply complicit in the contemporary form of alienation from selfhood that Kierkegaard called "aestheticism."

THE NIGHT IN WHICH ALL COWS ARE BLACK

THE ETHICAL SPHERE

Besides being concerned with the problem of boredom, the sophisticated aesthete was also concerned with the problem of freedom. The difficulty derives from the fact that the individual is forced to live in society, yet the demands that society places on the individual cause a loss of freedom. From the earliest moments society requires that the individual structure his or her behavior within certain more or less rigorous parameters, that he or she play typical behavior **ROLES**.

I WANNA PLAY.

FINE. YOU CAN BE A PILOT, A THIEF, A NEUROSURGEON, A BUM, A TIGHT-ROPE WALKER, A MAD BOMBER, A LION TAMER, OR PRESIDENT OF THE UNITED STATES.

I HAD IN MIND SOMETHING MORE LIKE RING-AROUND-THE-ROSY.

MY ROLE IS REDISTRIBUTOR OF THE WEALTH

There are professional roles, familial roles, character roles, and roles within roles. These roles are all typical ways of doing things. Most of them are socially useful, because they are agreed-upon formats for human interaction that eliminate misunderstanding, violence, and social collapse into anarchy.

However, there are some roles that are socially dysfunctional or pathological. Any one person inhabits many roles throughout the course of even a day (the salesperson, husband, father, chessplayer, church deacon, member of the PTA). Sometimes these roles are superimposed one upon the other, sometimes they overlap at the edges, sometimes they are contradictory. There are rules, conventions, procedures and formats for almost anything we can conceive of as a human action. Any activity that cannot be so analyzed appears irrational or even insane. (Yet irrationality and insanity themselves have certain typical components. Even unpredictability is predictable.) If the behaviorists were to be delighted by this discovery, Kierkegaard was horrified by it. It seemed to empty the word "self" of meaning. Roles are a kind of protective armor, but what do they protect? What if there is nothing inside the armor plating? We would like to think that the self is like an artichoke, whose layers of armor protect a "heart."

But what if the self is more like an onion, which has no heart? Is the self, like the onion, just the total of its protective coats? The aesthetic young author of the first volume of Kierkegaard's <u>Either/Or</u> (1843) countered this problem by furtively slipping from role to role in the most unpredictable manner (as did young Kierkegaard himself) thereby the aesthete hoped to achieve freedom, which he equated with lack of pre-dictability. For this, he was severely chastised by Kierkegaard's spokesman for the ethical realm, Judge Wilhelm, who accused the aesthete of flee-ing from the very freedom he claimed to seek.

The aesthete's self had been splintered into a multiplicity of mutually exclusive roles that, even though they were unpredictable, were nevertheless still dictated by society. The aesthete had deceived himself into believing that he was protecting and nurturing a self behind those roles. In fact, his self was nothing but a series of grotesque, inverted images in a broken mirror held up to social reality. The aesthete's self was more complicated than the self of the average person, but the aesthete's self too was exhausted in his roles.

Judge Wilhelm admonishes his aesthetic friend:

Life is a masquerade, you explain, and for you, this is inexhaustible material for amusement; and so far, no one has succeeded in knowing you; for every revelation you make is always an illusion,.... Your occupation consists in preserving your hiding-place, and that you succeed in doing, for your mask is the most enigmatical of all. **In fact, you are nothing: you are merely a relation to others, and what you are you are by virtue of this relation.**

Here we see the main problem of aestheticism, the fact that it is simply a perverse form of role playing. The aesthete's self is nothing but a series of meaningless masks, and even though the aesthete dons them as protests against society, they are still the creation of society.

Judge Wilhelm continues:

"Do you not know that there comes a midnight hour when everyone has to throw off his mask? Do you believe that life will always let itself be mocked? Do you think you can slip away a little before midnight in order to avoid this? Or are you not terrified by it?...

Or can you think of anything more frightful than that it might end with your nature being resolved into a multiplicity, that you really might become many, become, like those unhappy demoniacs, a legion, and thus you would have lost the inmost and holiest thing of all in a man, the unifying power of personality."

The reference to the demoniacs is an allusion to the possessed man in Luke 8: 32-37, who tells Jesus that his name is "Legion," and whose devils Jesus casts into a herd of swine, which then, in a mad frenzy, plunge headlong into a lake and are all drowned.

Like that unhappy herd, the aesthete's personality has been splintered into a disunifying force that allows these roles to cohere. Hence, the schizoid aesthete has no self.

If the aesthete has no self, how can he get one? Kierkegaard tells him, "CHOOSE THYSELF!" But how is this to be done? First of all, this act of choosing oneself is possible for the aesthete only when the rising tide of despair brings the individual to the "Either/Or," that explosive point where he passionately wills to be his true self and recognizes that such a wish entails willing the extinction of his old, sick self.

It is at this volatile moment of near derangement that one can make "THE LEAP." By the sheer force of his passion, the individual rips himself out of his old form of existence (aestheticism), and by losing his self, gains his self. For the first time in his miserable life the individual JUDGES himself from some perspective other than that of narcissistic hedonism.

(It is for this reason that Kierkegaard makes his spokesman the ethical judge.) As a result of the negative judgement he must pass on his old self, the new self begins to be constituted.

I FIND YOU **GUILTY** AS CHARGED

Judge Wilhelm writes:

My either/or does not in the first instance denote the choice between good and evil; it denotes the choice whereby one chooses good _and_ evil/or excludes them. Here the question is under what determinants one would contemplate the whole of existence and would himself live. . . . for the aesthetical is not evil, but neutrality. . . . It is, therefore, not so much a question of choosing between willing the good _or_ evil, as of choosing to will, but by this in turn the good and the evil are posited.

The choice that Kierkegaard's Judge Wilhelm describes here is not the selection of some particular ethical code; it is a more basic decision: whether to hold oneself responsible to an ethical code _at all_.

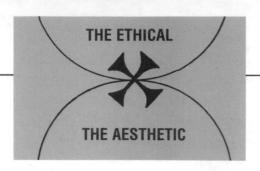

THE ETHICAL

THE AESTHETIC

This primordial moral decision is the X that marks the transition from the aesthetic realm to the ethical. Once one makes it, one has passed into the ethical, and one's selfhood can crystallize around the Either/Or. Of course, this X cannot remain abstract. It must be consummated with a particular commitment, but despite Kierkegaard's personal radical Christian commitment, there is nothing in his characterization that requires that this decision be exclusively Christian rather than Kantian, utilitarian, Buddhist, socialist, anarchist, or humanist. Any one of these would be a consistent consequence of the initial ethical choice that Kierkegaard requires as long as it fulfills these two imperatives: a commitment to self-perfection, and a commitment to other human beings. (Or perhaps to one other human being, such as Regina Olsen. Judge Wilhelm just happens to be married, and in Either/Or he carries on a long discourse on the virtues of marriage that is so idealized and so boring that it could in fact only have been written by someone who was not married.)

IT WOULD BE THE MORAL THING TO DO

BLAH-BLAH DRONE GAB DRONE DRONE

Once one has taken "the leap," that is, made the fundamental choice, then one <u>is</u> the project that follows from that choice. One has truly CHOSEN ONESELF. The individual's roles will no longer be fragmented, rather they will cohere by virtue of the fact that one's moral commitment will be expressed in each of these roles. Of course, one must still live in a society among other humans, therefore to a certain extent one's roles will still be socially dictated, but the self will be freely expressed even within the confines of the deterministic social system. Also, any of the roles that are incompatible with one's moral commitment will be discarded.

CAN ONE BE A CHRISTIAN <u>AND</u> A USED CAR SALESMAN?

Let us return to Judge Wilhelm one last time as he explains what is to be gained by "the choice."

> The choice itself is decisive for the content of the personality, through the choice the personality immerses itself in the thing chosen, and when it does not choose it withers away in consumption.

The picture that emerges is the following: The X that was the passionate decisiveness of self-judgement and that was the criterion of the ethical personality becomes the focal point around which the whole personality crystallizes.

Take a look at this diagram:

$$\frac{a}{b} \quad \frac{c}{d} \quad \frac{e}{f} \quad \frac{g}{h} \quad \frac{X}{Y} \quad \frac{i_x}{j_x} \quad \frac{k_x}{l_x} \quad \frac{m_x}{n_x} \quad \frac{o_x}{p_x}$$

Letters (a) through (h) symbolize the kinds of choices open to the aesthete: (a) either to breakfast on shredded wheat or (b) on puffed wheat; (c) either to write a poem or (d) go to the shore; (e) either to dress formally or (f) wear a T-shirt, and so on. Y represents the decision to remain morally neutral—that is, to remain in aestheticism, and it is a decision, either conscious or unconscious, that is presupposed in decisions (a) through (h).

X stands for the archetypal ethical choice, which, when made, predetermines all future choices as being choices that bear the unique mark of just that personality and not only of the role demanded by the particular circumstance.

Moreover, in a certain sense, every future choice will be an occasion for self-judgement. That is to say, every future situation will be a moral one. There will be no more moral neutrality. If the particular ethical stance taken by the individual is Christian, then upon entering any social situation whatsoever the individual must ask herself, "How shall Love be best served here?" The individual will judge herself in each situation and at each moment as either "Guilty/Not Guilty." Similarly, an individual who has chosen revolutionary Communism as her particular moral stance must ask, "How shall the Revolution be best served? How shall the human oppression of humans be combatted here?" And this person too will be "Guilty/Not Guilty."

It might be objected that the Christian and the Communist will still choose between breakfast cereals, just as the aesthete did, without these choices becoming "Christian" or "Communist." But Kierkegaard's point was that the aboriginal moral choice and its consummation in terms of a particular ethical code created a whole human world for the individual to inhabit and thereby defined all future situations as moral situations, so we might well ask here, would a true Christian or a true Communist, knowing that half the world's population goes to bed hungry, allow herself the indulgence of choosing between shredded wheat and puffed wheat? This inference from Kierkegaard's theory is justified despite the fact that Kierkegaard himself often indulged in choosing among fine brandies and cigars. He was not always capable of exemplifying the radical consequences of his own views.

THE
RELIGIOUS
SPHERE

Although Judge Wilhelm tells his aesthetic friend that the ethical involves a balance of the aesthetic, the moral and the religious, and despite his life being rather commonplace and even boring, there is nevertheless a certain harshness in Kierkegaard's ethical realm. The individual is engaged in a constant self-scrutiny and self-judgement from which there is no reprieve. It is almost more than one can bear. And indeed, Kierkegaard talks about an "ethical despair" that eventually brings the individual to his or her knees.

Perhaps this harshness was part of Kierkegaard's strategy to bring his reader to consider more seriously the religious sphere. In fact, Kierkegaard never really inhabited the ethical sphere as he describes it. He did not marry Regina. He later said that Either/Or, the book outlining the ethical, "was written in a monastery."

But don't think that the "leap" from the ethical sphere to the religious is an *escape* from harshness. Kierkegaard's religious realm is often a stark landscape.

Kierkegaard's religious views are subliminally spread across every page that he ever wrote. The most complete account of the religious sphere is found in his little masterpiece, <u>Fear</u> <u>and</u> <u>Trembling</u> (1843). This book, written under the pseudonym of Johannnes de silentio, purports to be an attempt to understand the biblical story of Abraham and Isaac. It is an intentionally unsuccessful attempt, for every interpretation Johannes tries to make fails. After many aborted efforts he finally cries out in despair:

ABRAHAM I CANNOT UNDERSTAND!

In fact, his failure to understand Abraham brings Johannes to suspect his own intellectual capacities, because he notices that almost everyone else seems to understand the story perfectly well. (Kierkegaardian irony showing through again, of course.) Let us briefly review the pertinent aspects of the story of Abraham as told in Genesis 11-12.

Abraham was a hereditary tribal leader of the Hebrews. Late in life he married his half-sister, Sarah, who was barren. When Abraham was seventy-five years old, God commanded him to take his people and begin a journey to a land that God would show him. God made a covenant with Abraham and promised him that Sarah would become the mother of a son who would be the father of a great nation. The years passed and Sarah did not conceive. Then when Abraham was ninety-nine and Sarah ninety, God appeared to Abraham again and renewed the promise.

Sarah conceived and gave birth to Isaac. The circumcision and the weaning of the child were celebrated with great joy by Abraham, who loved his son. Then came that terrible night described in Genesis 22: 1-2, when Abraham was awakened in the night by the voice of God, saying:

TAKE NOW THY SON, ISAAC; WHOM THOU LOVEST, AND GET THEE INTO THE LAND OF MORIAH; AND OFFER HIM THERE FOR A BURNT OFFERING UPON ONE OF THE MOUNTAINS WHICH I WILL TELL THEE OF.

Without hesitation and telling no one, Abraham took Isaac, travelled with him three days through that lonely desert, placed the boy on the appointed altar, lifted the sacrificial knife and was totally prepared to make the fatal thrust when the Angel of the Lord stopped him, saying that Abraham had passed the test, and allowing him to sacrifice in Isaac's place a ram that was conveniently caught in a nearby thicket. So Abraham got Isaac back, returned to his people, and lived in blessedness the rest of his days.

Johannes de silentio is stunned by this story. He tries to conceive of Abraham not as a mythical hero, but as a living man of flesh and blood. As such, Abraham is incomprehensible, but more than that, he is horrifying. He inspires in Johannes the "fear and trembling" of the title of Kierkegaard's book.

First, Abraham is incomprehensible because of his certainty. How can he be sure that he has correctly understood his mission?

Furthermore, Abraham is incomprehensible because of his power. Johannes asks:

Finally, Johannes is perplexed and horrified by Abraham because Abraham's act seems all too close to being an act of criminal insanity.

Now, all these factors might constitute a very good reason for simply ignoring the story of Abraham and Isaac. But Johannes cannot do this because it has always been considered as an exemplary case of faith (and Johannes is very interested in faith as a concept even though he himself is an unbeliever), and because we are told that "Abraham is the father of us all." Johannes suspects that if he could somehow reveal the secret of Abraham, he would fathom the human condition. So he is obsessed with the story and horrified by it at the same time. That is, he "dreads" it in Kierkegaard's sense—he has for it "a sympathetic antipathy and an antipathetic sympathy."

Despite the impenetrability of Abraham's case, it at least admits of a partial analysis, according to Johannes. He discovers that Abraham's act is a "double-movement," a "movement of infinite resignation," and a "movement of faith." The first is a negative element, in which Abraham gives up Isaac, and the second is a positive element in which Abraham gets Isaac back. The paradox for Johannes (and this is the paradox of faith) is that each of these elements occurs at the same time in the same act.

When Abraham makes the movement of infinite resignation (and thereby becomes what Kierkegaard calls "a knight of Infinite Resignation") he loses everything. He has "renounced fineness," which means he has renounced the world. He also seems to have renounced societal rights and obligations, and familial duties and love. He has renounced his position as a moral agent. When he takes Isaac into the desert and leaves Sarah behind, he has lost Isaac, Sarah, his past, his future, and his very self. (He has lost his self because at this point Abraham represents Kierkegaard's "ethical self"; so by renouncing morality, he renounces his self.) Furthermore, he is infinitely resigned to these losses.

Why would anyone ever want to make such a painful and difficult move? What is to be gained by it? Kierkegaard says, "what I gain is myself...and only then can there be any question of grasping existence by virtue of faith." And in a passage that could be the touchstone of all existentialism, Kierkegaard adds:

Infinite resignation is that shirt we read about in the old fable. The thread is spun under tears, the cloth bleached with tears, the shirt sewn with tears; but then too it is a better protection than iron and steel. .... The secret in life is that everyone must sew it for himself.

From these passages it can be seen that the X that is the transitional movement between the ethical and the religious is in many respects identical to the X that is the transition between the aesthetical and the ethical. In each case, one assumes the "lofty dignity which is assigned to each man, that of being his own censor, which is a far prouder title than that of Censor General to the whole Roman Republic."

IN EACH CASE, ONE GAINS A NEW SELF, BUT ONLY AT THE EXPENSE OF ONE'S OLD SELF.

The difference is that the second "leap" is more horrible, for in that first movement one fell away from one's old sick self, but in the second movement one falls away from humankind. Abraham must sacrifice Isaac as well as himself. Søren must sacrifice Regina as well as himself.

No surprise that in his own mind, Kierkegaard associates the story of Abraham and Isaac with the much-avoided passage in the New Testament:

"If any man cometh unto me and hateth not his own father and mother and wife and children and brethren and sisters, yea, and his own life also, he cannot be my disciple."

(Luke 14: 26)

According to Kierkegaard, the act of infinite resignation is a purely private existential project, and it cannot be justified nor made comprehensible within a social context. Indeed, one of the most disturbing aspects of the story of Abraham emerges when Johannes asks himself this question: WHAT IS THE RELATION OF ABRAHAM'S UNDERTAKING TO ETHICS, MORALITY AND LAW (all of which Kierkegaard calls "the universal")? Johannes answers in horror:

Abraham's whole action stands in no relation to the universal. . . . By his act he has overstepped the ethical entirely.

Abraham has annulled the ethical for what he takes to be a higher purpose. Kierkegaard calls this act of moral annulment a "TELEOLOGICAL SUSPENSION OF THE ETHICAL," and there can be no moral justification for such a suspension. "Abraham's relation to Isaac, ethically speaking, is quite simply expressed by saying that a father shall love his son more dearly than himself." Such a love is incompatible with being willing to kill one's son, even killing him "BY VIRTUE OF THE ABSURD," which, according to Johannes, was Abraham's motivation. It is this motive that is so perplexing to Johannes de silentio.

He is not only perplexed; at times he is positively outraged. He says, "Abraham enjoys honor and glory as the father of faith, whereas he ought to be prosecuted and convicted of murder." At one stage of his analysis, Johannes suspects that the honor that Abraham enjoys in the popular mind is due to a common misunderstanding of the story. Many say of Abraham, "The great thing was that he loved God so much that he was willing to sacrifice to Him his best."

Johannes imagines a preacher who eloquently presents his flock with just such a misleading interpretation of Abraham. One of his listeners is so moved by the sermon that he returns home and executes his son. The next Sunday the preacher thunders down on the man's empty pew, "O abominable man, offscouring of society, what devil possessed thee to want to murder thy son?" The point, of course, is that this is precisely the attitude that the preacher <u>should</u> have had toward Abraham. For Johannes the question is whether faith can make it "a holy act to be willing to murder one's son."

If not, Abraham is doomed. If so, we are faced with an irresolvable paradox, and for Kierkegaard, faith was just such a paradox. Let's move away from faith's negative forerunner, "infinite resignation," and look at the "movement of faith" itself.

According to Kierkegaard, at the same instant that Abraham made the movement of infinite resignation —and lost everything— he also made the movement of faith—and regained everything in a new way. Abraham thereby became "THE KNIGHT OF FAITH." He believed God's old promise. He believed that God would not require Isaac of him. This he

... believed by virtue of the absurd; for there could be no question of human calculation, and it was indeed absurd that God who required it of him should the next instant recall the requirement. He climbed the mountain. Even at the Instant the knife glittered he believed that God would not require Isaac.... He believed by virtue of the absurd; for all human reckoning had long since ceased to function.

So, it is Abraham's absurd motivation that makes him unintelligible to Johannes. The absurdity is not that Abraham believed that Isaac would be restored. (After all, Abraham had God's promise.) The absurdity is that Abraham had already given up Isaac infinitely and yet <u>at</u> <u>the</u> <u>same</u> <u>time</u> he believed that he would not have to give up Isaac. Abraham believed two mutually exclusive ideas at the same time and acted on these contradictory beliefs in the same project. Abraham is not simply incomprehensible, he is mad! Johannes does not hesitate to call Abraham insane. "Humanly speaking, he is crazy and cannot make himself intelligible to anyone. And yet it is the mildest expression, to say he is crazy."

However, the bare fact that Abraham is insane is not what astonishes Johannes. (Many people <u>are</u> insane, after all.) Rather, what is incomprehensible is that by virtue of his insanity, Abraham became the Father of Faith. There is an intangible dimension of Abraham's madness whereby he establishes an absolute relation to God, and becomes great thereby. Johannes praises Abraham in his lunacy, saying:

Abraham was greater than all, great by reason of his power whose strength is impotence, great by reason of his wisdom whose secret is foolishness, great by reason of his hope whose form is madness, great by reason of the love which is hatred of oneself.

Adopting a term from Plato, Kierkegaard calls Abraham's condition "divine madness." Kierkegaard, far from condemning Abraham's madness, advocates it. Now, he does not advocate it because it is madness, rather because it is divine. Abraham may be unintelligible to his fellow humans, but he is not unintelligible to God. Abraham "speaks a divine language…he 'speaks with tongues'."

Some readers of <u>Fear</u> <u>and</u> <u>Trembling</u>, remembering that Johannes de silentio is not a believer, maintain that Kierkegaard is not serious when he calls Abraham's condition "divine madness." Rather, it is claimed, Abraham only appears to be mad from the point of view of the non-religious. Well, Abraham certainly is unintelligible to the non-believer, but is it really the case that Abraham's fellow initiates in the religious realm understand him?

Johannes de silentio, at least, vehemently denies it, and there is little reason to doubt that he speaks for Kierkegaard when he says:

Faith is this paradox,... the individual cannot make himself intelligible to anybody. People imagine maybe that the individual can make himself intelligible to another individual in the same case. ...But the one knight of faith can render no aid to the other. Either the individual becomes a knight of faith by assuming the burden of the paradox, or he never becomes one. In these regions partnership is unthinkable.

The knight of faith cannot communicate with his fellow knight of faith because only God can judge whether the knight's madness

is divinely inspired and not demoniacal. Behaviorally, the two different types of lunacy appear the same. Kierkegaard's "Knight of Faith" is indeed left in "absolute isolation" on the desert of Moriah. It is not surprising, as one critic says, that Kierkegaard's severity has driven more people out of the religious sphere than into it. But Kierkegaard probably would not mind. Anyone who could be driven out of the religious sphere by rhetoric alone did not belong there in the first place.

A Postscript

$\mathcal{W}$hat about "Knights of Faith" in Kierkegaard's time, or in our own? What would they be like? Kierkegaard surprises us (and defuses some of the explosiveness of his own radical doctrine) by having Johannes de silentio tell us that they cannot be detected. Perhaps every third person we see is a Knight of Faith, for all we know. For they blend right in with everybody else. Who is the Knight of Faith? Perhaps, says Johannes, the postman, the shopkeeper, the tax collector, the teen-age girl next door. Behaviorally, they look just like everyone else. The difference is that they have already lost all worldly things to infinite resignation and gotten everything restored to them by faith. They are in the world, but not of it. —Perhaps one of them is even a cranky, eccentric writer named Søren Aabye Kierkegaard, who has lost his true love, Regina Olsen, to infinite resignation, but has absolute faith that she will be restored to him "by virtue of the absurd."

IN THE WORLD, BUT NOT OF IT

If Kierkegaard believed that of himself when he wrote <u>Fear</u> <u>and</u> <u>Trembling</u>, he had abandoned the idea by the time he wrote in his diary, "If I had faith, I would have remained with Regina," just as his direct attack on the frivolity and superficiality of the Danish Church in the last year of his life signaled the abandonment of his doctrine of indirect communication and of his view that the Knight of Faith could remain undetected in the crowd. When he passed out pamphlets in the streets of Copenhagen, Søren Kierkegaard, a true Knight of Faith, had sallied forth, and in losing, he won, just like that other Knight of Faith somewhere on the desert of La Mancha.

Glossary

(An asterisk [*] indicates terms that can be cross-referenced in the glossary.)

Absurd, The. Kierkegaard's religious hero, Abraham, acts "by virtue of the absurd" in that the reasons for his actions cannot be made intelligible. Abraham's faith takes over when "reasonable" reasons run out. For Kierkegaard, all existential decisions are absurd, because they are activations of both freedom* and faith,* and these transcend all systems of rationality. [See **Fear and Trembling**.]

Aestheticism. The life-mode of the person whose motivation is pleasure or sensation. (The term originates in the Greek word for "perception.") For Kierkegaard this is a sub-human form of existence, because it is ultimately a biological form. Even its most sophisticated variations, which try to convert sensualism into spirituality, fail and lead only to boredom, despair,* and a death-wish. [See **Either/Or**.]

Aesthetic Sphere, The. The whole world-view constituting a framework of reasoning, perception, motivation, and socialization guided by sensualism. [See **Either/Or**.]

Anguish. See **Dread**.

Anxiety. See **Dread**.

Bad Faith. As a technical philosophical term this phrase was coined by Kierkegaard's wayward twentieth-century disciple Jean-Paul Sartre. It is a paradoxical attempt at self-deception in which one denies and unsuccessfully tries to flee from one's freedom,* responsibility, and anguish.*

Behaviorism. A twentieth-century psychological theory, based on the work of John Watson and his disciple B.F. Skinner, according to which all accounts of human activity can and should be reduced to descriptions of bodily movements ("behaviors"). Kierkegaard's work is fervently anti-behavioristic, because it maintains the importance of an inner life ("sujectivity,"* "inwardness") that may not necessarily be externalized. E.g., the "knight of faith"* is radically different from others, but this difference cannot be detected by observing the "knight's" behavior. Of course, Kierkegaard's enemies are not Watson and Skinner, whom he pre-datcd, but G.W.F. Hegel, to whom Kierkegaard attributes the view that "the outward is the inward, and the inward is the outward."

Christendom. Kierkegaard's pejorative term for that which usually passes as Christianity,* but which in fact is only its outward trappings, disguising a complacent and comfortable institutional falsification of true Christianity. [See **Attack** **upon** **Christendom**.]

Christianity. Normally thought of as any of a number of variations of the religious doctrine that Jesus of Nazareth is the Son of God, and that belief in his divinity, imitation of his life, and practice of his ethical code may result in a divine judgement granting eternal life. However, Kierkegaard denies that Christianity is a doctrine at all. It is for him a form of "spirit," of "inwardness," a "cure" based on an absurd* faith* that, if achieved (always by individuals alone and never by group action), guarantees a form of passionate selfhood and authenticity with an eternal consciousness. [See **Training** **in** **Christianity**.]

Despair. The opposite of faith.* A loss of hope that is a failure to will the self that one truly is. Kierkegaard calls it "the sickness

unto death," because it embodies a desire for self-annihilation. [See **The Sickness unto Death**.]

Determinism. The view that there is no freedom,* rather that all is necessity. A view incorporated in B.F. Skinner's behaviorism* and implicated in Karl Marx's dialectical* materialism (according to which there are laws of history and economics that govern our lives) and in Sigmund Freud's psychoanalysis (according to which much of our behavior is determined by unconscious motives that are not in our control.) Determinism is thoroughly rejected by Kierkegaard, who makes freedom his basic category.

Dread (or **Anguish** or **Anxiety**, depending on the translation). A complex psychical category for Kierkegaard that is foundational of both consciousness and selfhood. It is the fear of one's own freedom,* a fear of "nothing" (because one's freedom is capable of making real that which is now non-existent). It is also a "sympathetic antipathy and an antipathetic sympathy"— a desire for what one fears and a fear of what one desires. Namely, it is sin (especially in the case of Adam and Eve). [See **The Concept of Dread**.]

Dialectic, The (or **Dialectical**). A term borrowed by Kierkegaard from G.W.F. Hegel according to which all individual ideas, objects, persons, events and historical periods are defined by their relationship of opposition-and-dependency to their own "otherness." The contradictory features of these relationships are resolved by acts of "mediation" where the oppositions are synthesized into a cohesive unity. Kierkegaard has a love/hate relationship with Hegel's "dialectic" (i.e., a dialectical relationship). He uses the notion continuously but rejects the idea of "mediation." Oppositions always remain and in fact are presupposed by the idea of freedom* and choice ("Either/or"). Only commitment and faith* ("by virtue of the absurd"*) can overcome opposition.

Divine Madness. A phrase Kierkegaard borrowed from Plato, who in <u>Phaedrus</u> has Socrates say, "the greatest of blessings come to us through madness, when it is sent as a gift of the Gods." Kierkegaard used the idea of "divine madness" in his journals and in at least six of his books. Its most developed presentation is in <u>Fear</u> and <u>Trembling</u>, where it designates the "madness" of the Patriarch Abraham, which is a form of faith* and is contrasted with its opposite, demoniacal madness.

Ethical Sphere, The. A whole world-view constituting a framework of reasoning, perception, motivation, and socialization guided by a devotion to "the ethical," that is, a passionate decision to judge oneself in terms of a universalizable* moral rule involving the quest for self-perfection and an absolute commitment to at least one other fellow human being. (One of Kierkegaard's pseudonyms says, "Through her [Regina?] I feel sympathy for every man.") [See **Either/Or**.]

Existentialism. A term coined by Jean-Paul Sartre to name his philosophy of the mid-1940s, inspired by the writings of Kierkegaard, who is now often called "the Father of Existentialism." A philosophy emphasizing radical freedom, responsibility, self-creation, individualism, subjectivity, and commitment. Following Kierkegaard's method of "indirect communication"* and "irony,"* many of existentialism's practioners have also been novelists (Sartre, Simone de Beauvoir, Albert Camus, Miguel de Unamuno), playwrights (Sartre, Unamuno, Gabriel Marcel), or at least have prioritized poetic discourse over philosophy and science (Martin Heidegger, Unamuno). Some great novelists have also been called existentialists (Fyoder Dostoyevsky, Franz Kafka).

Faith. See **Knight of Faith, The**.

Freedom. A key category in Kierkegaard's philosophy. But there are competing ideas of freedom. There is freedom as the availability of genuine alternatives ("either/or"), which in turn presupposes the idea of freedom as possibility. Here, freedom is opposed to actuality (that which is the case) and to necessity (that which must be the case). But there is also freedom as passionate commitment to a principle that one chooses as one's personal law—that is to say, acting on the "either/or." The aesthete's* error is in seeking freedom exclusively in infinite possibility, which precludes freedom as commitment. By leaving all possibilities infinitely open, he abolishes his own "either/or." [See **Either/Or**.]

Golden Mean, The. Aristotle's ideal in his search for virtuous action. The "golden mean" is a path of virtue found half-way between excess and deficit. E.g., in the case of the correct attitude in the presence of an enemy, the deficit is cowardice and the excess is fool-hardiness. The golden mean in this case is courage. But this path of virtue is an experimental one. It cannot be established with a mathematical formula. Kierkegaard's quest for authentic selfhood is similarly experimental.

Hedonism. The philosophy which claims that pleasure is the highest value. Historically associated with Epicurus in Greece in the third century B.C. and with Thomas Hobbes in the seventeenth century. Kierkegaard's aesthete* is a hedonist. [See **Either/Or**.]

Indirect Communication. The only mode of communicating "subjective truths,"* according to Kierkegaard, involving the use of philosophical irony* and pseudonymous authorship, whose goal is to create a rhetorical environment in which the reader's normal assumptions are pulverized, creating a clearing in which he or she can find his or her own subjective truth. [See **Concluding Unscientific Postscript**.]

Irony. In Kierkegaard, closely related to indirect communication.* A form of discourse in which the expression of the message is incongruous with the content of the message. Sometimes the literal meaning is the direct opposite of the intended meaning. The use of poetry, oxymoron, parody, sarcasm, understatement, overstatement, and even falsehood to communicate a message that must be interpreted by inverting the apparent meaning. All of Kierkegaard's pseudonymous works are ironic and must be interpreted (which is why there are plausible readings of Kierkegaard that are very different from the one in this book). [See **The Concept of Irony**.]

Knight of Faith, The. Kierkegaard's term for the individual who has lost the finite world in an act of "infinite resignation*" and has recovered it in a simultaneous act of faith, an act that is carried out by virtue of the absurd,* and thereby the individual has placed him or herself directly in the religious sphere.* [See **Fear and Trembling**.]

Knight of Infinite Resignation, The. Kierkegaard's term for the individual who has given up the finite world as a philosophical act of self-recovery. By giving up worldliness the individual who makes the move of infinite resignation destroys the world's power over the individual and places him- or herself in a position of self-definition. A prelude to becoming a Knight of Faith*. [See **Fear and Trembling**.]

Law (or **Principle**) **of Identity, The**. One of the three foundational principles of logic, according to Aristotle, founder of the science of logic. "X (where X can stand for anything) is identical to itself." "X=X." E.g., "'It is raining in Athens' equals 'It is raining in Athens'." If the three foundational principles are false, nothing else can be true, according to Aristotle. Yet Hegel wants to abolish them, thinks Kierkegaard, and replace them with a new dialectical* logic.

Law (or **Principle**) **of the Excluded Middle, The**. One of the three foundational principles of logic according to Aristotle. (See also **The Law of Identity*** and **The Law of Non-Contradiction***). According to the law of the excluded middle, "It is the case that either X or not -X." "X v ~X." E.g., once we've agreed on the meaning of "Athens" and of "rain," then "Either it is raining in Athens, or it is not raining in Athens." No third possibility exists.

Law (or **Principle**) **of Non-Contradiction, The**. One of the three foundational principles of logic according to Aristotle. (See also **The Law of Identity*** and **The Law of the Excluded Middle***). According to the law of non-contradiction, "It is not the case that Y is true of X and at the same time Y is not true of X." "~(X. ~X)." E.g., "It is not the case that 'it is raining in Athens' and 'it is not raining in Athens' at the same moment."

Leap, The. The moment of passion when one moves from one sphere of existence (e.g., the ethical*) to another (e.g., the religious*) by suddenly putting behind oneself one's old self. This leap is performed "by virtue of the absurd,* " because all the old criteria of rationality have themselves been left behind. Kierkegaard quotes an unidentified German poet: "Ein seliger Sprung in die Ewigkeit"— a blessed leap into eternity.

Lutheranism. The Protestant religious movement based on the teachings of Martin Luther (1483-1546), a monk who broke with the Catholic Church when he nailed his ninety-five theses to the door of the church at Wittenburg, demanding reform of the church, including abandonment of the system of indulgences, elimination of ecclesiastical corruption, and punishment for abuses of church power. Ultimately, Luther denied the validity of the idea of the Papacy (denouncing the current pope as the Devil), abolished the hierarchy of priests, married a nun, and put vernacular translations of the Bible in the hands of the peasants. Lutheranism was the official Church of Denmark in Kierkegaard's day, but Kierkegaard came to the conclusion that it had strayed far from the true Christianity.*
[See **Attack upon Christendom**.*]

Monasticism. The medieval solution to the problem of the temptations of the world. Individuals, becoming monks or nuns, would renounce the world and remove themselves from it, remaining behind the high walls of monasteries of convents, often in remote locations, adhering to a strict order of discipline and devotion. This is not Kierkegaard's solution to the problem of worldliness, and he criticizes it. His solution (at least at one point in his life) is the "double movement" of Faith and Infinite resignation.* The "Knight of Faith"* lives among other humans. Abraham returns to his village. Kierkegaard lives in an expensive apartment in Copenhagen.

THE WHIRLED IS CUMIN TO AND EN

New Testament, The. A compilation of writings added to the Jewish Bible (viz., to the "Old Testament") by the early Christian* church, comprising the four "Gospels" (Matthew, Mark, Luke, and John), the "Acts of the Apostles" (a description of the events that befell Peter, John, Stephen and Paul after the crucifixion), the "Epistles" (letters of St. Paul to various Christian communities in the Mediterranean

basin), and the "Revelations of St. John the Divine" (prophecies of the end of time). The New Testament is believed by Christians to demonstrate that Jesus of Nazareth is the Christ, i.e., that He is the Messiah prophesied in the Old Testament.

Objective Truth. Truth for which there are public tests or criteria that can be applied identically by more than one person. E.g., the truths of mathematics, science, or history. Although objective truths are not completely objective for Kierkegaard (because all knowledge contains an element of belief), they differ from "subjective truths"* in that the emphasis of objective truth is on the truth of the <u>content</u> of the assertion rather than on the truth of the personal response to it. Kierkegaard accepts that there are objective truths (i.e., that math, science, and history are possible) but insists that they are "essentially indifferent" to human existence. In an existential sense, they do not matter. [See **Concluding Unscientific Postscript**.]

Pietism. A fundamentalistic form of Lutheranism* that stressed personal piety and an acute awareness of sin over doctrine and ritual. Kierkegaard's father, Michael, was raised in this tradition.

Religious Sphere, The. A whole-world view constituting a framework of reasoning, perception, motivation, and socialization guided by a devotion to the divine. In <u>Concluding Unscientific Postscript,</u> Kierkegaard further divides this sphere into "religiousness A" (those features of religious life that all religions have in common) and "religiousness B," a religion of paradox that is recognizable to the reader as Kierkegaard's idea of true Christianity.* Religiousness "B" presupposes "A", but not vice-versa. [See **Concluding Unscientific Postscript** and **Fear and Trembling**.]

Surd. Originally from the Latin word <u>surdus</u> meaning "deaf," designates an inexpressable quality or an irrational residue. That which is still left over when all analysis is complete. Together with the prefix <u>ab</u> meaning "from" or "away from" producing "ab-surd,"* roughly, out of that which cannot be voiced or heard. Existence is for Kierkegaard a "surd."

Subjective Truth. A private truth, a truth for which one can live or die. These are not truths about facts, but about values, or about the foundational categories that ground both facts and values for an individual. Here, unlike the case of "objective truth,"* there are no public criteria to which one can appeal, and subjective truths cannot be communicated except indirectly (see also **Indirect Communication***), because each individual must learn these truths individually from him-or herself. [See **Concluding Unscientific Postscript**.]

Synoptic Gospels, The. The first three books of the New Testament* ("Matthew, Mark, and Luke,) where we are given firsthand, eye-witness accounts, one slightly differing from the other in detail and emphasis, of the teaching and activity of Jesus of Nazareth during the last four or five years of his life. They are quoted more by Kierkegaard than are other parts of the Bible, though he takes some of his inspiration from the "Epistles" of St. Paul and from the Old Testament.

Teleological Suspension of the Ethical, The. The annulment of the universal * demands of ethics in the name of a purpose that is higher than these demands. Kierkegaard asks whether such a suspension of moral duty could ever be justified (since just such a teleological suspension of the ethical apparently was required by God of the biblical Patriarch, Abraham, the Father of us all). Kierkegaard's paradoxical answer, or lack thereof, is a main topic in what he took to be his best book. [See **Fear and Trembling**.]

Universal, The. There are at least two different ways Kierkegaard uses this term. (A) In his theory of language, "the universal" designates general concepts embodied in language that are necessarily abstracted out of (and therefore away from) experience. E.g., every individual leaf is different from every other individual leaf, but in order to be able to communicate we must have nouns, verbs, adjectives, adverbs, etc. that suppress all individual differences and find some abstract quality that all leaves are meant to have in common. The result is that language and thought, being universal, always alienate us from actual experience, which is particular. [See **Johannes de Climacus, Or De omnibus dubitandum**.] (B) In his moral theory, derived from Kant and Hegel, "the universal" designates those actions that can be universalized, i.e., generalized without contradiction. (E.g., honesty can be univeralized, but lying cannot. It is logically impossible to conceive of everyone always lying. If everyone always lies, there are no lies.) This is the Kantian side. For Hegel, achieving "the universal" is the moral goal of the individual, but achieving that goal requires the suppression of one's own individuality for the higher good of family, community, state and humanity. When Kierkegaard asks whether there can be a "teleological suspension of the ethical,"* he is asking whether there is any justification for suspending "the universal" in the name of a purely individual (hence unintelligible) purpose. [See **Fear and Trembling**.]

Bibliography

I. Kierkegaard's main works in English Translation

(Danish publication dates in brackets. Asterisks indicate pseudonyms under which Kierkegaard published.)

The Concept of Irony. Trans. Lee M. Capel, Bloomington, Indiana: Indiana University Press, 1968. [1841.]

Either/Or, Vols. I & II. Trans. David F. Swenson and Lillian Marvin Swenson, Garden City, N.Y.: Doubleday Anchor Books, 1959. [1843, edited by Victor Eremita*, Vol. I written by "A," * Vol. II written by "B," a.k.a. Judge Wilhelm.*]
also
Either/Or. Trans. Howard V. Hong and Edna H. Hong, Princeton, N.J.: Princeton University Press, 1987.

Fear and Trembling (with The Sickness unto Death). Trans. Walter Lowrie, Garden City, N.Y.: Doubleday Anchor Books, 1954. [1843, Johannes de silentio*]
also
Fear and Trembling (with Repitition). Trans. Howard V. Hong and Edna H. Hong, Princeton, N.J.: Princeton University Press, 1983.
also
Fear and Trembling. Trans. Alastair Hannay, New York: Penguin Books, 1985.

Repitition (with Fear and Trembling). Trans. Howard V. Hong and Edna H. Hong, Princeton, N.J.: Princeton University Press, 1983. [1843, Constantin Constantius.*]

Johannes Climacus, or De Omnibus Dubitandum Est. Trans. T.H. Croxall, London: Adam & Charles Black, 1958. [1842-1843, published posthumously, Johannes Climacus.*]

Philosophical Fragments. Trans. David Swenson and Howard V. Hong, Princeton, N.J.: Princeton University Press, 1967. [1844, Johannes Climacus.*]

The Concept of Dread. Trans. Walter Lowrie, Princeton, N.J.: Princeton University Press, 1957. [1844, Vigilius Haufniensis.*]
                also
The Concept of Anxiety. Trans. Reidar Thomte and Albert B. Anderson, Princeton, N.J.: Princeton University Press, 1980.

Stages on Life's Way. Trans. Walter Lowrie, N.Y.: Shocken Books, 1967. [1845, William Afham,* Judge Wilhelm,* Frater Taciturnus,* Quidam,* edited by Hilarius Bookbinder.*]

The Present Age. Trans. Alexander Dru, New York: Harper Torchbooks, 1962. [1846]

Concluding Unscientific Postscript. Trans. David F. Swenson and Walter Lowrie, Princeton, N.J.: Princeton University Press, 1960. [1846, Johannes Climacus.*]

Works of Love. Trans. Howard V. Hong and Edna H. Hong, New York: Harper Torchbooks, 1964. [1847]

Purity of Heart Is to Will One Thing. Trans. Douglas V. Steere, New York: Harper Torchbooks, 1956. [1847]

The Point of View for My Work as an Author. Trans. Walter Lowrie, ed. Benjamin Nelson, New York: Harper Torchbooks, 1962. [1848, published posthumously.]

The Sickness unto Death (with Fear and Trembling). Trans. Walter Lowrie, Garden City, N.Y.: Doubleday Anchor Books. [1849, Anti-Climacus.*]
   also
The Sickness unto Death. Trans. Howard V. Hong and Edna H. Hong, Princeton, N.J.: Princeton University Press, 1980.

Training in Christianity. Trans. Walter Lowrie, Princeton, N.J.: Princeton University Press, 1944. [1850, Anti-Climacus.*]
   also
Practice in Christianity. Trans. Howard V. Hong and Edna H. Hong, Princeton, N.J.: Princeton University Press, 1991.

Attack upon Christendom. Trans. Walter Lowrie, Boston, Beacon Press, 1959. [1854-1855.]

The Journals of Kierkegaard, 1834-1854. Trans. and ed. Alexander Dru, London: Fontana Books, 1969.

The Last Years: Journals 1853-1855. Trans. and ed. Ronald Gregor Smith, London: Fontana Library, 1968.

II. **Kierkegaard's Philosophy Anthologized.**
A. **Kierkegaard Anthology.** Ed. Robert Bretall, Princeton, N.J.: Princeton University Press, 1973.

III. **Recommended Secondary Sources.**

Agacinski, Sylviane. **Aparte:** Conceptions and Deaths of Søren Kierkegaard. Trans. Kevin Mewmark, Tallahassee: Florida State University Press, 1988.

Collins, James. **The Mind of Kierkegaard.** Princeton, N.J.: Princeton University Press, 1983.

Gardiner, Patrick. **Kierkegaard**. Oxford: Oxford University Press, 1988.

Hannay, Alastair. **Kierkegaard**. London: Routledge and Kegan Paul, 1982.

Lowrie, Walter. **A Short Life of Kierkegaard**. Garden City, N.Y.: Doubleday Anchor, 1961.

Mackey, Louis. **Kierkegaard: A Kind of Poet**. Pittsburgh: University of Pennsylvania Press, 1971.

Malantschuk, Gregor. **Kierkegaard's Thought**. Princeton, N.J.: Princeton University Press, 1989.

McDonald, William. **Kierkegaard and Post-Modernism**. Tallahassee: Florida State University Press, 1989.

Mooney, Edward F., **Knights of Faith and Resignation: Reading Kierkegaard's <u>Fear</u> <u>and</u> <u>Trembling</u>**. Albany, N.Y.: State University of New York Press, 1991.

Perkins, Robert. **Kierkegaard's <u>Fear</u> <u>and</u> <u>Trembling</u>: Critical Appraisals**. Birmingham: University of Alabama Press, 1981.

Taylor, Mark C. **Kierkegaard's Pseudonymous Authorship: A Study in Time and the Self**. Princeton, N.J.: Princeton University Press, 1975.

Thompson, Josiah. **The Lonely Labyrinth: Kierkegaard's Pseudonymous Works**. Carbondale, Il.: Southern Illinois University Press, 1967.

Thompson, Josiah, ed. **Kierkegaard: A Collection of Critical Essays**. Garden City, N.Y.: Anchor Books, 1972.

Sources of Quoted Passages

From the Works of Søren Kierkegaard

KEY

AuC= **Attack upon Christendom**. Trans. Walter Lowrie, Boston: Beacon Press, 1959.

CoD= **The Concept of Dread**. Trans. Walter Lowrie, Princeton, N.J.: Princeton University Press, 1957

CoI= **The Concept of Irony.** Trans. Lee M. Capel, Bloomington, Indiana: Indiana University Press, 1968.

CuP= **Concluding Unscientific Postscript**. Trans. David F. Swenson and Walter Lowrie, Princeton, N.J.: Princeton University Press, 1960.

E= **Either/Or, Vol. I**. Trans. David F. Swenson and Lillian Marvin Swenson, Garden City, N.Y.: Doubleday Anchor Books, 1959.

F&T= **Fear and Trembling**. Trans. Walter Lowrie, Garden City, N.Y.: Doubleday Anchor Books, 1954.

JC= **Johannes Climacus, Or De Omnibus Dubitandum Est**. Trans. T.H. Croxall, London: Adam & Charles Black, 1958.

JoK= **The Journals of Kierkegaard, 1834-1854**. Trans. and ed. Alexander Dru, London: Fontana Books, 1969.

O= **Either/Or, Vol. II**. Trans. David F. Swenson and Lillian Marvin Swenson, Garden City, N.Y.: Doubleday Anchor Books, 1959.

PoV= **The Point of View for My Work as an Author**. Trans. Walter Lowrie, ed. Benjamin Nelson, New York: Harper Torchbooks, 1962.

SuD= **The Sickness unto Death**. Trans. Walter Lowrie, Garden City, N.Y.: Doubleday Anchor Books, 1954.

The left column designates page numbers from <u>Kierkegaard</u> <u>For</u> <u>Beginners</u>. The right column designates page numbers from Kierkegaard's works keyed on p. 141. First and last words from each quotation are listed.

7	"Who is it?...bad to him?"	TiC	176
7	"As a child...crazy upbringing."	PoV	76
10	"God had vetoed the marriage."	JoK	73
11	"If I had...with Regina."	JoK	86
16	"Abracadabra...secret of 'Christendom' "	AuC	212
16	"One cannot live...off of it."	AuC	182
16	"This has to...God as a fool."	AuC	59
23	"approached each...away empty handed."	Col	199
26	"In the...relation to them."	CuP	551
34	"Truth is subjectivity."	CuP	169
37	"All decisiveness...in subjectivity."	CuP	207
37	"Only in...to be in error."	CuP	214
39	"nothingness that pervades being."	CuP	75
42	"the possibility...at any moment"	CuP	76
43	"You can count...cannot come."	CuP	88
44	"who woke up...he was dead."	CuP	149
46	"deceiving his...into the truth."	PoV	39
46	"throw this book down."	O	172
52	"cannot consciousness...produces, duplicity."	JC	148-9
59	"However deep...object of dread."	CoD	101
60	"One may...become dizzy."	CoD	55
61	"Dread is...antipathetic sympathy."	CoD	38
65	"Man is spirit...not yet a self."	SuD	146
67	"Such a derived...itself to another."	SuD	146-7
70	"willing to be...one truly is."	SuD	153
70	"The Torment...able to die."	SuD	150
71	"because he...cannot become nothing."	SuD	151
71	"the more consciousness...the despair."	SuD	175
72	"Thus when the...rid of himself."	SuD	151-2
72	"a blind door...is nothing."	SuD	189
73	"sits as it were...to be itself."	SuD	196
75	"He rages...misery from him."	SuD	206
80	"This species...by the score."	E	284
81	"Of all ridiculous...I laugh heartily."	E	24
85	"Boredom is the...upper hand."	E	282
86	"either die of boredom...(the active form)."	E	285
87	"You go to see...part of a book."	E	295

DREAD IS A SYMPATHETIC ANTIPATHY AND AN ANTIPATHETIC SYMPATHY

Index

ANGUISH

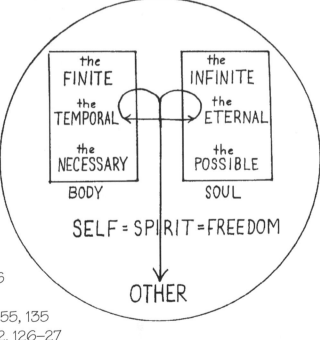

IF YOU LIKED KIERKEGAARD...

SUBSTITUTE!

And knowledge, as you will discover in our "Documentary Comic Books," is fun! Each book is painstakingly researched, humorously written and illustrated in whatever style best suits the subject at hand.

Making complex subjects simple **and serious subjects** fun!!!

That's **Writers and Readers**, where *For Beginners*™ books began! Remember, if it doesn't say...

Writers and Readers ——●

... it's not an <u>original</u> *For Beginners*™ book!

Chomsky For Beginners

by David Cogswell; illustrated by Paul Gordon

Race For Beginners

by S.E. Anderson Illustrated by The Cro-Mat Collective

McLuhan For Beginners

by W. Terrence Gordon; illustrated by Susan Willmarth

I-Ching For Beginners

by Brandon Toropov; illustrated by John Kane

Eastern Europe For Beginners

by Beck, Mast and Tapper